Showing Up For Democracy

Break Through Doubt, Leverage the Popular Vote, and Shape Our Future

Bonnie A Ross

Bigger Than Me

Contents

I dedicate this book to my mother, Marian L. Ross, whose mornings began with a simple yet powerful act—raising the American flag outside our door. Through her, I inherited a deep appreciation for the wit and wisdom of Abraham Lincoln, a gift that continues to inspire me every day.

Introduction: How Oprah, Elizabeth Warren, and Indivisible Inspired This Book

I've always believed in the power of democracy—not the glossy, idealized version we learn about in school, but the messy, loud, and often frustrating reality of it. It's a system built on the idea that people with wildly different perspectives can come together to hash out their differences and figure out how to move forward. It's beautiful in its imperfection, but for a long time, I wasn't sure how I could make a real difference within it.

That changed after the 2024 presidential election. The results weren't shocking, but the wave of disillusionment that followed caught me off guard. I heard it everywhere: friends, neighbors, and even strangers lamenting that their voices didn't matter, that the system was broken, and that showing up made no difference. It wasn't just apathy; it was a resignation so deep it felt immovable. Their words lingered with me, not just because I understood their frustration, but because a part of me had felt that way, too.

Not long after, I came across a story Oprah Winfrey shared. She talked about a friend who lived in a solid blue state and decided not to vote because she felt her vote wouldn't change anything. "Why bother?" her friend had said. That simple phrase struck a nerve. How many people had convinced themselves of that same thing? How many elections, policies, and futures had been shaped by that mindset? I couldn't stop thinking about it.

Then came the moment that changed everything. I attended an online meeting hosted by the founders of Indivisible and Senator

Elizabeth Warren. I didn't know what to expect, but the energy was electric. These weren't people lamenting the state of the world; they were focused on solutions, on action, on the incredible power of ordinary people to shape extraordinary change. They shared stories of small acts—writing letters to representatives, organizing neighborhood meetings, having conversations with friends—that snowballed into movements that couldn't be ignored. It was a rallying cry, not just for the system but for the potential of the people in it.

As I logged off that night, I couldn't sit still. I started scribbling ideas in my notebook, and one question rose above the rest: What if I could be the person who helped others see the power of showing up? What if I could take everything I'd just learned and make it accessible to anyone who had ever felt small or powerless in the face of national politics?

That's where this book began. I wanted to strip away the intimidation of civic engagement, to demystify the process, and to remind people of the joy in being part of something bigger. But I knew that writing wasn't enough. I wanted to create tools that made it easy to get involved. That's when BiggerThanMe.info was born—a platform where anyone can learn about federal policies and send pre-written letters to their representatives. No guesswork, no overwhelm—just a simple, direct way to make your voice heard.

The truth is, democracy doesn't thrive on perfection. It doesn't need heroes or grand gestures; it needs people willing to show up, one small step at a time. Oprah's story reminded me how easy it is to feel invisible. Indivisible and Senator Warren reminded me how powerful it is to take that first step anyway. And here I am, passing the torch to you.

If you've ever wondered where to start, I hope this book becomes your map. If you've ever felt like your voice doesn't matter, I hope you find in these pages the proof that it does. And if you've ever doubted whether change is possible, I hope you'll remember this: change begins with you. It begins when we show up—together.

With gratitude, hope, and just the right amount of stubbornness,

Bonnie

Powered by Engaged Citizens
BiggerThanMe.info

1

The Popular Vote—Your Voice, Your Power

I f you've ever felt like your vote doesn't matter, you're not alone. It's easy to feel small in the face of a political system that seems to prioritize everything but the everyday people it's supposed to serve. Headlines about voter suppression, political gridlock, and billionaires influencing elections only add to the frustration. But what if I told you that your vote—yes, yours—is one of the most powerful tools we have to shape the world around us?

The popular vote isn't just about numbers on a screen on election night. It's about your voice, your priorities, and your vision for the future. It's about millions of people coming together to say, "This is what we care about, and this is what we stand for." It's not just politics—it's personal.

Let me bust one of the biggest myths right now: "My vote doesn't count." That's simply not true. History is filled with moments that prove otherwise. In 1960, John F. Kennedy won the presidency by less than 0.2% of the popular vote—about one vote per neighborhood. In 2000, George W. Bush became president because of just 537 votes in Florida. And in a local school board election in

Rhode Island, a literal coin toss decided the winner after a tie. One more vote would have changed the outcome. Still think your vote doesn't matter? These examples show that even the smallest actions can create ripples that change the course of history.

But here's the thing about voting: it's not just about the outcome of a single election. It's about sending a message that resonates far beyond the ballot box. When you vote, you're saying, "I care about what happens in my community. I want leaders who listen to us. I'm not letting someone else make this decision for me." Your vote adds to a chorus of voices that leaders can't ignore. Whether it's about climate change, healthcare, education, or criminal justice reform, the issues you care about gain momentum when they're backed by the power of the popular vote.

And even if your candidate doesn't win, your vote still matters. It shapes the debate, influences policies, and sets the stage for future change. Democracy isn't perfect—it's messy, frustrating, and often slow. But that doesn't mean it's not worth fighting for. Apathy only strengthens the forces that benefit from disengagement. Real change doesn't happen overnight; it's the result of millions of small acts—like casting a vote—stacking up over time.

Think of democracy as a garden. Each vote is a seed. It might not grow immediately, but with care, attention, and collective effort, those seeds bloom into something powerful—a community, a movement, a better future.

And the numbers back this up. At the local level, voter turnout has a 90% impact on the outcomes of city council races, school board elections, and mayoral contests. These decisions shape education, public safety, and infrastructure—the things we experience every day. State elections follow closely, with a 75% impact, steering critical issues like healthcare access, education funding, and economic policy. Nationally, the popular vote serves as a barometer for public opinion, setting mandates that guide leaders' priorities. Even in presidential elections, where the Electoral College complicates things, the popular vote still influences legitimacy and governance.

Looking at the Numbers

Did I mention I'm a realist? That means I love numbers and graphics—the kind that strip away fluff and show the heart of the matter. Let's take a look at a graph does exactly that, breaking down the impact of the popular vote across different aspects of the political process. It's a clear, data-driven look at how our collective participation translates into action, from local elections to national mandates. Let's unpack what these numbers mean and why they matter.

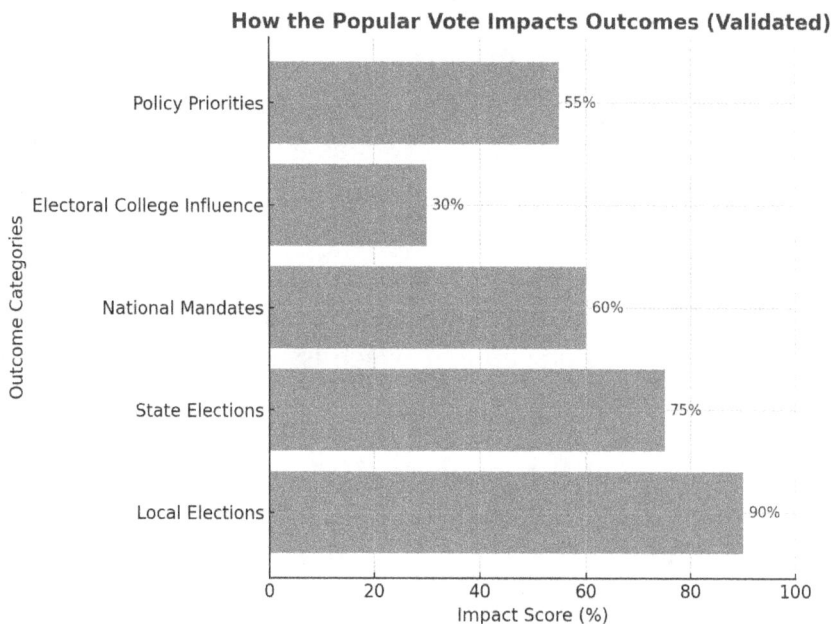

How the Popular Vote Impacts Outcomes (Validated)

Outcome Category	Impact Score (%)
Policy Priorities	55%
Electoral College Influence	30%
National Mandates	60%
State Elections	75%
Local Elections	90%

Sources: Local & State Election Rules (90% & 75% based on direct determination by votes), Electoral College Limitations (30% based on symbolic influence), National Mandates & Policy Priorities (60% & 55% based on historical trends).
Definitions: Impact Score reflects direct and indirect influence of popular vote in respective domains.

- Local Elections (90% Impact) – At the local level, the popular vote is king. With a 90% impact, these elections—city councils, school boards, mayors—are directly determined by voter turnout. This is where your ballot has the most immediate and visible effect, influencing decisions on education, public safety, and infrastructure that shape everyday life. If you want to see democracy in action, look no further than your local polling place.[1]

- State Elections (75% Impact) – State elections follow closely behind with a 75% impact. Here, the popular vote holds significant sway in electing governors, state legislators, and deciding on ballot measures. While factors like gerrymandering can slightly dilute this influence, a strong voter turnout can often overcome these challenges. These elections steer critical issues such as healthcare access, education funding, and state-level economic policy, making them a vital area for participation.[2]

- National Mandates (60% Impact) – On the national stage, the popular vote plays a pivotal role, though it's less direct. With a 60% impact, it serves as a barometer for public opinion, setting mandates that guide leaders' priorities. It shapes the narrative, signaling to policymakers what the electorate values most. Even when it doesn't directly determine outcomes, the popular vote influences what policies are pursued and which issues dominate the national conversation.[3]

- Electoral College Influence (30% Impact) – Presidential elections are a unique case, with the Electoral College limiting the direct impact of the popular vote to 30%. However, this doesn't render the popular vote insignificant. A strong showing can enhance the perceived legitimacy of the winner and influence their ability to govern effectively. Over time, it can also fuel momentum for systemic reforms, ensuring the popular vote remains a cornerstone of the democratic process.[4]

- Policy Priorities (55% Impact) – Finally, the popular vote has a 55% impact on shaping policy priorities. Voting trends illuminate what issues matter most to the public, from climate change to economic justice. Elected officials look to these patterns to align their agendas with voter demands. While actual implementation depends on political will and external pressures, the popular vote is a driving force in determining which issues rise to the forefront.[5]

Why This Matters Now

If you're reading this, you probably care about the world you live in. Maybe you're frustrated by how things are, or maybe you're hopeful for what could be. Either way, the truth is the same: democracy doesn't work on autopilot. It needs us—our voices, our actions, and yes, our votes. Every time you show up, you're refusing to hand over your power. You're reminding the system—and yourself—that your voice matters. And when millions of us do this together, the impact is undeniable.

Imagine your vote as part of a ripple in a pond. Alone, it might feel small. But when it joins thousands, millions of other ripples? It becomes a wave. A wave that can topple barriers, reshape policies, and hold leaders accountable. That's the power of the popular vote. That's the power of you.

So, the next time someone tells you that voting doesn't matter, tell them this: "One vote might not seem like much, but it's everything when we all show up together." Because democracy isn't about perfection. It's about participation. And it's about showing up—even when it feels hard, even when it feels small—because that's how change begins.

Concluding Thoughts

At its core, democracy is a powerful but fragile thing—one that thrives when we show up and falters when we don't. Voting isn't just a right; it's an opportunity to shape the world we want to live in. It's an act of hope, a statement of values, and a reminder that each of us has a role to play in creating a better future.

It's easy to feel overwhelmed by the enormity of the issues we face or cynical about the imperfections of the system. But democracy doesn't need perfection—it needs participation. It's about small, consistent actions that build over time into something much bigger than any one of us. And it starts with showing up, not just for ourselves, but for our communities and future generations.

Your vote is more than a drop in the ocean—it's part of a ripple that can become a wave. By casting your ballot, you're declaring that your voice matters, that your priorities deserve to be heard, and that you refuse to sit on the sidelines. Whether it's a local school board election or a national race, your vote contributes to a collective vision of progress and possibility.

So the next time you doubt the impact of your voice, remember this: every movement for change began with people like you deciding to act. Every victory started with someone believing it was worth the effort. And every step you take toward engaging in democracy helps strengthen the foundation for a brighter, more inclusive future.

Democracy isn't just something we inherit—it's something we build. Together. One vote at a time.

How Change Begins

The story of the 19th Amendment is a testament to how change begins—with a single voice, a small idea, and the courage to challenge the status quo. For decades, women across the United States fought for their right to vote, often facing ridicule, resistance, and even violence. Yet they persisted, believing that equality was not just an ideal but a necessity.

It began with voices like Susan B. Anthony, Elizabeth Cady Stanton, and Ida B. Wells, who planted the seeds of change by organizing conventions, delivering fiery speeches, and inspiring others to join their cause. Slowly, their message spread, growing into a movement fueled by marches, petitions, and relentless advocacy. At its heart were ordinary people—mothers, daughters, sisters, and friends—who refused to accept a world where their voices didn't count.

As public support grew, so did pressure on lawmakers to act. State by state, the tide began to turn, with women winning the right to vote in local elections. This momentum culminated in Congress passing the 19th Amendment in 1919, but one final hurdle remained: it needed ratification by three-fourths of the states.

The decisive moment came in Tennessee in 1920, where the legislature was deadlocked. The fate of the amendment rested on the shoulders of Harry Burn, a young legislator expected to vote against it. But change often begins in unexpected places. Burn received a letter from his mother urging him to "be a good boy" and support women's suffrage. Her quiet yet powerful plea tipped the scales, and he cast the deciding vote to ratify the amendment.

This victory wasn't the end of the journey but the beginning of a new chapter in democracy. It showed that change doesn't happen overnight—it starts with individuals brave enough to take the first step, movements willing to fight for their vision, and the collective will of people who believe in something greater than themselves. From one voice to a nation transformed, the story of the 19th Amendment reminds us that change begins when we dare to imagine a better world—and act to make it real.

2

Why Showing Up Matters

S howing up—it sounds simple, almost too simple, but it's one of the most impactful actions we can take. Showing up declares, "This matters." Whether it's cheering a friend at their first nerve-wracking open mic night or walking into a daunting Monday morning meeting, your presence holds power.

The same is true for democracy. Showing up for yourself, your community, and the future you envision is one of the clearest ways to effect change. Yet doubts creep in: Does my voice matter? Can my actions make a difference? These questions are familiar and valid.

At times, democracy feels sluggish and overwhelming. The problems seem vast, and the system can feel unresponsive. Yet, showing up is not about solving everything at once or expecting seismic shifts from a single effort. It's about being part of a collective momentum—a movement that builds strength over time.

There's power in being counted. Think about the joy of hearing your name called by a friend or having your coffee order remembered by a barista—it affirms your existence and value. In democracy, voting and civic participation achieve a similar effect.

When you cast a ballot, attend a meeting, or volunteer, you assert, "I'm here, and my voice matters." And when enough people make this declaration, the ripple effects are undeniable. Policies shift. Leaders take notice. Communities rally. The reverse is also true: when people don't show up, decisions are made without them, often by those who may not share their values or priorities.

Democracy is personal, but it's also collective. When you vote or advocate for change, it's not just about your concerns—it's about standing up for others. Think about those who can't vote: children whose futures hinge on today's policies or immigrants striving for citizenship. Showing up is an act of solidarity, amplifying voices that might otherwise go unheard. Your actions become part of a larger movement, weaving together countless individual efforts into a powerful force for progress.

Voting is not the final destination; it's the catalyst. A high voter turnout sets the stage for advocacy groups to thrive, signals to leaders that people are paying attention, and highlights critical issues for future campaigns. Every ballot cast strengthens the democratic process, reminding everyone involved that citizens care deeply about the direction of their communities and nation.

Choosing not to participate doesn't halt the wheels of democracy—it just hands control to others. History reminds us that disengagement often enables harmful policies and neglects pressing issues. Silence is never neutral; it's a missed opportunity to influence the future.

Cynicism about democracy is understandable—slow processes, frustration, and setbacks abound. But disengagement doesn't foster improvement. Showing up, whether by voting, attending local meetings, or voicing concerns to representatives, is how trust is rebuilt and accountability is established. As more people engage, it becomes harder for leaders to ignore critical issues or evade scrutiny. Democracy thrives on this active participation.

Democracy isn't about grand gestures—it's about steady, deliberate actions. A quick email to your representative, a conversation with a friend, or even taking five minutes to research an issue adds up. Change is slow, messy, and imperfect, but it begins when individuals commit to showing up consistently.

Concluding Thoughts

At its heart, democracy is about showing up. It's about contributing, even when the steps feel small, and trusting that those steps create ripples of progress. When you show up, you declare, "I care, this matters, and I'm part of this." Your voice becomes part of a broader conversation, shaping policies, holding leaders accountable, and steering us toward the future we all hope for.

Every movement begins with people deciding to show up. So, the next time you wonder if your vote or action matters, remember: real change starts with you—and it starts when you show up.

How Change Begins

In 1969, a small group of young people gathered on the polluted banks of the Cuyahoga River in Cleveland, Ohio. The river, infamous for being so polluted that it had caught fire multiple times, symbolized the environmental crisis of the time. But this particular gathering wasn't just to protest—it was to organize. They wanted the country to pay attention to the environmental destruction happening around them

One of those young activists, Dennis Hayes, had a vision for something bigger. Inspired by the anti-war teach-ins of the 1960s, he proposed a national day of environmental action. With the support of Senator Gaylord Nelson and thousands of grassroots organizers, Hayes helped create the first Earth Day on April 22, 1970.

What started as an idea turned into a massive demonstration, with over 20 million Americans participating. Students held rallies, communities cleaned up rivers and parks, and people of all backgrounds came together to demand change. The event was a turning point—it led directly to the creation of the Environmental Protection Agency (EPA) and landmark legislation like the Clean Water Act and Clean Air Act.

The success of Earth Day wasn't about one dramatic act. It was about showing up—millions of people, in their own communities, taking action to demand a healthier, cleaner future. It proved that when people come together, even the most entrenched problems can start to change.

The story of Earth Day reminds us that showing up doesn't always have immediate results, but it plants the seeds for lasting change. One river, one rally, one conversation at a time—it's how movements begin and grow into something powerful enough to reshape the future.

3

Top 10 Myths About Elections and Democracy

E lections come with their fair share of myths—ideas so baked into our collective understanding that they start to feel like truths. But here's the reality: a lot of these myths are just noise, distracting us from what really matters.

We've all heard them: *"Your vote doesn't matter," "All politicians are corrupt,"* or the ever-popular *"Character doesn't count as long as they get the job done."* These myths aren't just harmless misunder-standings—they can make the democratic process feel pointless, frustrating, or, worse, something only other people need to care about.

Let's bust some of these myths wide open, laugh at the absurdity of it all, and remind ourselves why democracy is worth showing up for.

Myth 1: My Vote Doesn't Matter

This one is a classic. It's the myth that just won't die, popping up every election season like that one mosquito you can never quite catch. The thinking goes something like this: "I'm one person. My vote won't change anything." But here's the deal: elections, especially at the local level, are often decided by razor-thin margins. And I mean *thin*.

There are elections that have literally come down to a handful of votes. There's even a story about a race being decided by drawing names out of a bowl—yes, an actual *bowl*.

So, while your vote might feel like one drop in a bucket, remember: buckets are filled one drop at a time.

Myth 2: Polls Tell You Who's Going to Win

Polls are like horoscopes: fun to look at, occasionally accurate, but not something you should plan your life around.

Sure, polling can give us a snapshot of public opinion, but it's just that—a snapshot. Polls can't predict late-deciding voters, turnout, or that unexpected surge of energy from people who didn't even tell their mom they were voting.

Remember, elections are decided by actual voters showing up, not by a percentage on a poll. And if you've ever seen a "90% chance of rain" forecast on a sunny day, you know exactly why polls aren't the whole story.

Myth 3: The Electoral College Means the Popular Vote Doesn't Matter

The Electoral College can make democracy feel like a game with confusing rules, but don't let it trick you into thinking the popular vote is useless.

The truth is, the popular vote matters—big time. It shapes political narratives, influences policy agendas, and lets leaders know what the majority of people care about. Even in presidential elections, where the Electoral College complicates things, a strong popular vote sends a powerful message that can ripple through the entire political system.

And don't forget, most elections—state, local, and congressional—are decided entirely by the popular vote. It's not perfect, but it's ours.

Myth 4: All Politicians Are Crooked

Ah, the "all politicians are the worst" myth. This one is as old as politics itself, and while we've all seen examples of leaders who don't exactly inspire confidence (*cough* shady scandals *cough*), it's important not to paint everyone with the same brush.

Most people who go into public service genuinely want to make a difference. Yes, politics can attract egos and bad actors (what industry doesn't?), but it also attracts thoughtful, hardworking people who care deeply about their communities.

This myth is so persistent because scandal and corruption make headlines. No one's rushing to cover the city councilmember who spent their Saturday fixing potholes or the state representative who quietly got a bill passed to fund local schools. But those people exist—and they're often the backbone of democracy.

If we assume all politicians are crooked, we risk giving up on the system entirely. And who benefits when that happens? Not us.

Myth 5: Character Doesn't Matter as Long as They Get the Job Done

This one's tricky because it sounds practical. The argument goes, "I don't care about their personal life or how they treat people, as long as they deliver results." But here's the catch: character and leadership are inseparable.

A leader's character shapes their decision-making, how they handle pressure, and whether they prioritize public good over personal gain. Leaders with integrity are more likely to listen to their constituents, work collaboratively, and admit when they're wrong. Leaders without it? Well, let's just say their "results" often come with strings attached.

The myth that character doesn't matter thrives because it's easier than holding leaders accountable. But democracy deserves better—and so do we.

Myth 6: Social Media Drives Elections

Social media is like the karaoke of democracy: loud, often entertaining, but rarely the main event.

Sure, platforms like Twitter and Instagram can amplify messages and get people talking, but they're not where most voters make their decisions. Seeing a viral post might make you chuckle (or groan), but it's not the same as researching candidates or discussing policies with friends.

If elections were decided by likes and retweets, we'd all be living under the rule of funny cat videos. (Honestly, not the worst idea.)

Myth 7: Debates Decide Elections

Debates are like the political Oscars: full of drama, memorable moments, and questionable fashion choices. But do they actually decide elections? Not really.

Most voters have already made up their minds by the time debates roll around. Debates are more about solidifying opinions than changing them. And while a zinger or gaffe might make headlines, it's not likely to shift the outcome.

Debates are entertaining, sure, but let's not confuse them with the main event. They're the popcorn at the movie theater—not the movie itself.

Myth 8: Scandals Always Sink Candidates

Scandals are like car crashes on the highway—people slow down to gawk, but they don't always change where they're going.

While some scandals are big enough to derail a career, most don't have the impact we think they do. Voters are surprisingly resilient when it comes to forgiving mistakes, especially if they see a candidate as aligned with their values.

The bottom line? Scandals grab headlines, but policies and priorities win elections.

Myth 9: Only Presidential Elections Matter

Presidential elections are the rockstars of democracy—they get the bright lights, the big crowds, and all the press. But if you ignore local and state elections, you're missing out on where the real action happens.

Your city council, school board, and state legislature aren't just deciding what's happening in your backyard—they're shaping the pipeline of future leaders. These local races are the talent scouting grounds of democracy. The people you vote for in your state legislature today could be running for Congress, or even the presidency, in the years to come.

Think about it: every national leader started somewhere. Barack Obama was once a state senator. Stacey Abrams built her career in Georgia's House of Representatives. Local elections don't just shape your community—they shape the feeder system for national talent. If you want a government that reflects your values at every level, it starts right here, at home.

And beyond that, local officials decide things that hit closest to home: how your schools are funded, whether your roads get fixed, and whether that proposed dog park finally becomes a reality. They might not get the big headlines, but they're the ones shaping your daily life—and paving the way for future leaders who can make a broader impact.

Skipping these elections is like skipping the opening acts at a concert and only showing up for the headliner. Sure, the main act is exciting, but the earlier performances are where you find the raw, developing talent that could become your favorite someday.

Myth 10: You Need to Be a Political Expert to Vote

This one is the most intimidating myth of all, and it's completely false. You don't need to know every policy detail or follow every debate to cast a meaningful vote.

Think of voting like ordering at a restaurant. You don't need to know how every dish is made—just what you're in the mood for. Focus on the issues that matter to you, do a little research, and trust your instincts.

Democracy isn't about perfection. It's about showing up.

Bonus Myth: American flag is associated with a single political party

The American flag, with its 13 stripes and 50 stars, symbolizes the unity and ideals of the United States: liberty, justice, and equality. However, a persistent myth associates this iconic emblem with a single political party. This misconception has grown in recent decades, fueled by partisanship, cultural symbolism, and media representation.

The myth stems from the flag's increasing visibility at events and rallies linked to specific political movements. Over time, one political party or ideological group adopting the flag as a backdrop or central icon in its events has unintentionally conveyed ownership of its symbolism. This trend has left some Americans feeling that the flag aligns with a singular political ideology, rather than representing the nation's diverse spectrum of beliefs.

In truth, the American flag does not belong to any political party. It is a unifying symbol intended to represent all citizens, regardless of their political leanings. The flag embodies the democratic principles enshrined in the Constitution, serving as a reminder of the sacrifices made by those who fought for the country's independence and the rights of its people.

Federal guidelines, as outlined in the U.S. Flag Code, emphasize the flag's role as a nonpartisan emblem. The code provides rules for its respectful display and use, emphasizing unity and reverence, not political division.

Politicizing the flag risks alienating citizens who may feel excluded from its symbolism. Such a division undermines the flag's purpose as a unifying force. When a national symbol is monopolized by a specific group, it ceases to reflect the collective identity and values of the nation as a whole.

To dispel the myth, we can actively embrace the flag as a shared symbol. This involves displaying it with pride across all communities, fostering education about its historical significance, and reframing its use as a representation of collective ideals rather than partisan stances.

By reclaiming the American flag as a nonpartisan emblem, the nation can move toward bridging divides and reaffirming its commitment to unity. The flag's stars and stripes are meant to represent "one nation, under God, indivisible, with liberty and justice for all"—a promise that transcends political affiliations.

Concluding Thoughts

The myths about elections are loud, persistent, and, frankly, pretty entertaining when you stop to think about them. But here's the truth: what really matters is participation.

Forget the scandals, the polls, and the endless social media chatter. Focus on what's real—your voice, your priorities, and your ability to shape the future. Because democracy isn't about the noise; it's about what we do together.

How Change Begins

Let's bust the myth that "polls tell you who's going to win." For that, we need to revisit the infamous 1948 presidential election between Harry S. Truman and Thomas Dewey—a race where the polls didn't just mislead voters; they almost rewrote history.

Throughout the campaign, polls consistently predicted Dewey, the Republican challenger, as the clear winner. Newspapers, pundits, and even some in Truman's own party were so convinced of

Dewey's victory that they treated it as a foregone conclusion. The Chicago Tribune even went to press early on election night with the now-iconic headline: "Dewey Defeats Truman."

But here's the twist: they were wrong.

While Dewey ran a cautious, scripted campaign, Truman hit the road, embarking on a 22,000-mile whistle-stop tour across the country. He visited small towns, spoke directly to voters, and connected with people who felt ignored by the political elite. Truman's relentless effort paid off—he won the election in a stunning upset that left pollsters scrambling to explain how they'd gotten it so wrong.

The problem was that the polls relied on outdated methods and assumptions, missing late-deciding voters and the energy Truman's campaign had sparked in the final weeks. The result? A glaring reminder that polls are snapshots, not crystal balls.

Truman's victory wasn't just a win for his campaign—it was a win for democracy. It showed that elections are decided by voters, not projections. The lesson is clear: don't let polls convince you to stay home. They might set the narrative, but they don't cast the ballots. Your vote matters, no matter what the numbers say beforehand.

This tale proves that showing up is what truly counts. Polls may make predictions, but voters make history.

4

Deciding Who Deserves Your Vote

Deciding who to vote for can feel overwhelming. Campaign ads, social media debates, and yard signs are everywhere, and it's easy to feel lost in the noise. At its heart, though, the question is simple: "Who aligns with the values and priorities that matter most to me?" Here's the good news: voting doesn't have to feel like a chore. When you focus on what's meaningful to you, the process transforms into an empowering conversation about your vision for the future. This chapter is here to guide you through that journey, helping you cut through the distractions and focus on what truly matters.

No candidate is perfect—they're human, after all. But that doesn't mean you can't find someone who champions the issues closest to your heart. Begin by identifying the topics that resonate deeply with you. Is it affordable healthcare because your last doctor's visit cost more than your rent? Climate action because the summers feel hotter and more unpredictable every year? Or maybe it's about ensuring your local schools have the resources they need to help every child thrive. Whatever it is, write it down. When you know what matters most to you, it's easier to spot candidates who share your priorities. You don't need to know everything about every candidate—just focus on the issues that hit home for you. Think of it like dating: find the one who matches your non-negotiables, not someone who ticks every single box.

Leadership isn't just about policies—it's about trust, vision, and integrity. A great leader listens, learns, and evolves with their community's needs. They don't pretend to have all the answers but are willing to collaborate, adapt, and work for progress. When evaluating candidates, consider whether their policies and past actions align with your values. Are they focused on solutions, or do they thrive on division? Do they admit mistakes and adjust, or do they deflect blame? At the end of the day, trust your instincts. A leader who feels genuine and informed is more likely to navigate challenges with integrity and focus.

Campaigns can feel like reality TV—flashy, emotional, and full of soundbites. But real leadership isn't about theatrics. It's about action. If a candidate has held office, their voting record is a powerful lens into their priorities. For newcomers, detailed platforms and public appearances offer insights into their plans and values. Take the time to look beyond polished ads and viral moments. What they've done—or plan to do—matters more than what they say in the spotlight.

It's just as important to notice what doesn't feel right. Watch for inconsistencies between a candidate's words and actions. Do they shift positions depending on the audience? Are they willing to take responsibility for mistakes, or do they dodge tough questions? Do they focus on scapegoating and fear, or are they working to build bridges? Trust is the foundation of effective leadership. A candidate who plays fast and loose with the truth or divides rather than unites will not reliably have your community's best interests at heart.

No candidate will align with every one of your beliefs—and that's okay. Democracy isn't about finding someone perfect; it's about choosing leaders who will move the needle in the right direction, even if it's one step at a time. Your vote is a powerful statement about your priorities and your vision for the future. By starting with what matters most to you, staying informed, and tuning out the noise, you're not just casting a ballot—you're shaping the kind of world you want to live in.

Concluding Thoughts

The act of choosing a candidate is more than just marking a ballot—it's an opportunity to express your values and shape the world you want to live in. It's not about finding someone who perfectly aligns with every belief or ideal; it's about identifying the leaders who will listen, learn, and take meaningful steps toward progress. This process isn't about perfection—it's about participating.

Democracy thrives when we engage with curiosity, clarity, and conviction. By focusing on what matters most to you, looking beyond the noise, and evaluating candidates through their actions and integrity, you empower yourself to make a thoughtful choice. Each vote contributes to the collective voice that drives change, setting the stage for the policies and priorities that shape our communities and our future.

Your vote is more than a number—it's a reflection of hope, a declaration of your vision, and a step toward creating a better tomorrow. Trust your instincts, honor your values, and know that by showing up, you are playing a crucial role in strengthening democracy. The world we want begins with the choices we make today. So choose boldly, vote with intention, and let your voice be heard.

How Change Begins

In the late 1800s, the United States faced a political and moral reckoning. The country was emerging from the shadow of the Civil War, but corruption gripped the government. "Boss" systems controlled cities, patronage ruled politics, and scandals like the Crédit Mobilier affair and the Whiskey Ring eroded public trust. For many Americans, it felt like integrity in leadership was a lost cause.

Enter Rutherford B. Hayes, a relatively obscure former governor of Ohio and Civil War general. Hayes wasn't flashy or charismatic, but he was deeply committed to reform and rebuilding trust in government. During the contentious presidential election of 1876, his character became a key reason he was chosen to run on the Republican ticket. The election was one of the most controversial in U.S. history, with disputes over electoral votes threatening to plunge the country back into chaos.

Hayes ultimately won the presidency after a painstaking compromise — but he didn't squander the moment. Instead, he focused on restoring integrity to the government. He refused to use patronage to reward supporters, angering many in his own party but staying true to his principles. He worked to reform the civil service system, laying the groundwork for future anti-corruption efforts.

Hayes also pushed for reconciliation between the North and South, though his policies were far from perfect. What set him apart was his willingness to prioritize the long-term health of the nation over short-term political gain.

Hayes' presidency marked a turning point, showing that leadership rooted in integrity could rebuild trust, even during divisive times. While his tenure wasn't without flaws, his commitment to ethical governance inspired future leaders like Theodore Roosevelt to carry the torch of reform.

This story reminds us why integrity in leadership matters. Electing people who value honesty, accountability, and collaboration doesn't just benefit the present—it shapes the foundation for generations to come. Change begins not with grand gestures, but with leaders who choose to do what's right, even when it's hard. And it all starts with the choices we make in the voting booth.

5

Impressions Are Not Facts

W e live in a world flooded with impressions—quick takes, eye-catching headlines, viral soundbites, and the curated perfection of social media feeds. They're everywhere, shaping our understanding in seconds. But here's the truth: impressions are rarely the full picture. They're like cotton candy—delightful at first glance, but not what you'd call a meal.

Our brains love shortcuts. First impressions save time and energy, helping us make quick judgments. But democracy isn't about speed—it's about care and consideration. A headline that declares a politician "saving puppies" or "destroying healthcare" might grab your attention, but the real story is often buried beneath layers of context. Take a moment to step back. Is the source credible? What's missing? First impressions might offer a spark, but only deeper understanding can light the way to informed choices.

Today's influencers are modern-day advertisers, blending relatability with persuasion. They feel like friends sharing advice, but let's not forget—they're often paid to influence. This doesn't mean all influencers are insincere; many genuinely care about the causes they promote. However, their motivations and messages should be approached with curiosity. Ask yourself: Who's funding this? What's the agenda?

One reason impressions stick is their emotional pull. A headline that fuels anger or fear is more likely to go viral than a balanced explanation. Why? Emotions are powerful drivers. But here's the catch: decisions made in the heat of emotion rarely serve us well. Next time you feel a strong reaction to something you read, pause and reflect: What's the goal of this message? Is it urging you to think—or just react?

In a world demanding constant attention, slowing down feels like rebellion. But it's also how we reclaim clarity. If a headline seems too dramatic or simplistic, dig deeper. Nuance lives beyond the clickbait. Check the source—does it come from a credible outlet or a cousin's blog post? Follow the money and ask, "Who benefits if I believe this?" Understanding motives helps uncover the truth. Think of this process as putting on a pair of glasses—it sharpens your view of reality.

When we let impressions guide us, we risk empowering those who aim to manipulate. But when we approach information with care, we contribute to a stronger democracy. Small acts—fact-checking, pausing before sharing, questioning motives—create ripples of informed engagement. Together, they add up to a culture of thoughtful participation.

Impressions are easy, fast, and flashy—but democracy thrives on thoughtfulness. Take the time to understand what's real. Ask questions. Look deeper. It's not about being the loudest voice in the room—it's about being the most informed. Because when we take the time to discern the truth, we're not just making better decisions—we're strengthening the foundation of our democracy. And that is always worth the effort.

Concluding Thoughts

In a world where quick impressions dominate and emotional re-actions are often amplified, choosing to pause and reflect is an act of courage. It's tempting to take headlines at face value, trust the polished words of influencers, or let our emotions dictate what we believe. But democracy, at its core, asks us to go deeper. It invites us to question, to think critically, and to engage with curiosity instead of assumptions.

Taking the time to understand what's real isn't always easy—it requires effort, patience, and sometimes the willingness to admit we don't have all the answers. But the rewards are profound. By seeking truth, we empower ourselves to make informed decisions that honor the complexity of our world. We strengthen not only our individual understanding but also the democratic process itself, contributing to a culture where truth and thoughtfulness prevail.

So, as you move through the endless stream of headlines, sound-bites, and viral posts, remember this: impressions may catch your attention, but they don't have to capture your trust. Take a breath. Ask the questions. Seek the story beyond the surface. Because when we choose thoughtfulness over immediacy, we're not just shaping a better democracy—we're building a stronger, more con-nected world. And that's a future worth working toward

How Change Begins

In 1934, California was a state on edge. The Great Depression had devastated lives, leaving unemployment and poverty in its wake. Amid the despair, Upton Sinclair, a muckraking author famous for The Jungle, stepped forward with a bold vision. Running for governor, Sinclair proposed his End Poverty in California (EPIC) plan, a sweeping agenda of cooperative farms, job creation, and progressive taxation. To many, his ideas symbolized hope—a way to start rebuilding lives and communities.

But to powerful business interests and political elites, Sinclair's campaign was a threat. His EPIC plan challenged the status quo, and instead of debating his policies, his opponents launched a different kind of attack. They didn't engage with facts or offer alternative solutions. Instead, they leaned into impressions, leveraging fear and emotional manipulation to derail his campaign.

For the first time in U.S. history, Hollywood was weaponized in a political race. Opponents funded fake newsreels that played in movie theaters across California, posing as legitimate journalism. These propaganda clips featured actors portraying everyday citizens—farmers, workers, and small business owners—denouncing Sinclair as a dangerous radical. Some claimed his policies would ruin their lives, while others warned of a flood of communists entering the state if he won. With stirring music and stark imagery, these newsreels left lasting impressions that stuck with voters long after the credits rolled.

Newspapers joined in, amplifying the campaign with sensational headlines and editorials that portrayed Sinclair as un-American. The result? Voters were swept up in fear, swayed by the emotional appeal of the propaganda, and disconnected from the reality of Sinclair's proposals. He lost the election to Frank Merriam, whose campaign offered little vision for change but relied on reinforcing the comfortable status quo.

The 1934 campaign serves as a cautionary tale about the dangers of shortcuts in democracy. It's tempting to trust what's easy and immediate—a dramatic headline, a viral clip, or a cleverly crafted ad—but those shortcuts often come at the expense of truth. Change begins not with impressions but with understanding.

Democracy isn't about emotional manipulation or flashy marketing; it's about taking the time to ask questions, dig deeper, and focus on what's real.

While Sinclair lost, his campaign ignited conversations about economic reform and social justice that reverberated long after the election. People began questioning the influence of propaganda and demanding more transparency in politics. Change didn't come all at once, but the seeds were planted.

The lesson here? Change begins with thoughtful engagement. It starts when we reject the easy answers and take the time to understand what's real. It begins when we refuse to be hijacked by fear and instead make decisions rooted in truth, empathy, and vision. So the next time you're scrolling through headlines or watching the latest political ad, pause. Ask questions. Dig deeper. Because every step toward understanding is a step toward meaningful change—and that's how democracy moves forward.

6
Building Your Information Toolkit

I n today's swirling sea of information, finding clarity feels like searching for a steady beam of light in the fog. But the truth is, we each hold the power to navigate this complexity. Building a personal information toolkit is more than a tool for staying informed—it's a shield against manipulation and a bridge to meaningful civic engagement. Reliable sources are your compass, guiding you toward understanding and empowering you to act with confidence.

Not all sources deserve your trust. Some shine brightly, offering well-researched, balanced insights that illuminate the path forward. Others? They lead us astray, chasing clicks and sowing confusion. The difference lies in their commitment to truth—an anchor in an age of swirling opinions.

Reliable sources earn your trust through their integrity. They are transparent about their authorship and funding, meticulously cite evidence, and strive for balance, even when navigating controversial topics. They admit mistakes and make corrections. These marks of reliability aren't just guidelines—they are lifelines in the quest for truth.

On the flip side, unreliable sources often prey on emotions, using fear and outrage to cloud judgment. Sensational headlines, unsupported claims, and divisive rhetoric are their tools. They distract, mislead, and undermine the critical thinking that democracy depends on. Spotting these warning signs isn't just a skill—it's an act of resistance against the tide of misinformation.

What Are the Marks of a Reliable Source?

A reliable source provides accurate, well-researched, and unbiased information. Here's what to look for:

- **Credibility:** Is the source established and respected? Reputable outlets like The Associated Press, BBC, or NPR have a track record of rigorous reporting and journalistic integrity.

- **Transparency:** Reliable sources clearly outline who they are, how they're funded, and what their goals are. If a website hides its authorship or funding, that's a red flag.

- **Fact-Based Reporting:** Good journalism backs claims with evidence, cites sources, and avoids sensationalism. Look for detailed, verifiable information instead of vague assertions.

- **Balanced Perspective:** While no source is entirely free of bias, trustworthy outlets strive to present multiple sides of an issue. Beware of sources that consistently lean too far in one direction without acknowledging opposing viewpoints.

- **Accountability:** Reliable sources issue corrections when they make mistakes. If a publication refuses to admit errors or doubles down on false claims, it's not trustworthy.

Source Redflags and Considerations

An unreliable source often prioritizes sensationalism, opinion, or profit over accuracy. Here are some warning signs:

- **Clickbait Headlines:** If the headline is designed to shock or outrage, but the article doesn't back it up with credible evidence, it's likely clickbait.

- **Lack of Evidence:** Watch out for sweeping claims without data or sources to support them. "Trust me" isn't good enough.

- **Emotional Manipulation:** Unreliable sources often use fear, anger, or outrage to provoke a reaction, bypassing critical thinking. There are legitimate news stories that will be upsetting. However, if the point of the story is to fill you with anger or anxiety, look for another source to balance this reporting.

- **Anonymous or Hidden Authors:** If you can't determine who wrote the content or where the information came from, approach with caution.

- **Agenda-Driven Content:** Some outlets exist solely to push a political or ideological narrative. While having a perspective isn't inherently bad, ignoring facts to support that narrative is. Pay attention to the tone of the piece. Is it neutral, or does it seek to divide, us vs. them theme? Who are the "us" and "them." A quality source seeks to inform, not divide.

- **Poor Writing Quality:** Frequent grammar errors, misspellings, or amateurish presentation can indicate a lack of professionalism and accountability.

Building Your Toolkit of Reliable Sources

An information toolkit is your personal compass in the vast, often overwhelming landscape of modern news and media. It's a carefully curated collection of reliable sources and strategies that empowers you to cut through the noise, discern truth from fiction, and make informed decisions. In a world awash with opinions, half-truths, and outright misinformation, your toolkit becomes a powerful ally, equipping you to stay grounded, confident, and engaged.

Creating your information toolkit isn't just about gathering links or bookmarking websites—it's a deliberate process of selecting diverse and trustworthy resources. Start by identifying core sources with a reputation for rigorous journalism, like major news outlets known for balanced reporting and fact-checking platforms that separate fact from fiction. Local news outlets bring vital community issues into focus, while niche sources provide specialized insights into areas like science, health, or policy. Aggregators can simplify your search by presenting multiple viewpoints on the same topic, offering a clearer picture of complex issues. Here's how to get started:

- **Establish Core News Sources:** Reputable outlets like The Associated Press, Reuters, and The New York Times are excellent for factual, in-depth coverage.

- **Use Fact-Checking Sites:** Incorporate resources like Snopes, PolitiFact, and FactCheck.org into your routine to verify claims and debunk misinformation. There are also browser plugins like Google Fact Check Explorer and NewsGuard that adds credibility ratings to news websites.

- **Diversify Your Perspectives:** Relying on just one or two sources can create blind spots. Include outlets with different editorial leanings to get a well-rounded view of the issues.

- **Explore Local News:** Don't overlook local journalism. Local papers and radio stations often provide valuable insights into community-specific issues.

- **Supplement with Niche Expertise:** For specialized topics like science, health, or finance, turn to organizations with subject-matter expertise, such as the CDC for health information, ProPublica for investigative journalism, or the Democracy Docket for legal updates.

- **Aggregators – Simplifying Reliable News Consumption:** Aggregators compile news from various sources, saving readers time. Platforms like The Ground aim to present multiple viewpoints on the same issue helping users see the full picture. By offering a range of sources aggregators help counteract the echo chamber effect.

How to Use Your Toolkit

Your information toolkit is a powerful resource, but its value depends entirely on how you use it. Here's a step-by-step guide to making the most of it, ensuring you stay informed, focused, and resilient in today's fast-paced media environment.

1. Verify Before Believing

When a major story breaks, resist the impulse to accept the first headline you see. Instead:

- **Cross-Check Sources:** Look at multiple trusted outlets to identify consistent facts.

- **Identify Common Threads:** Focus on details that appear across reliable sources—they're often the most credible.

- **Stay Skeptical:** If a claim seems exaggerated, overly convenient, or shocking, question it. Skepticism isn't negativity; it's a safeguard for accuracy.

2. Question the Narrative

Even reputable sources can falter. Stay proactive:

- **Check Evidence:** Does the article provide data, expert opinions, or citations? If not, dig deeper.

- **Be Mindful of Bias:** Understand that all sources have perspectives. Look for coverage from different angles to get a balanced view.

- **Avoid Confirmation Bias:** Challenge yourself to read sources that don't always align with your beliefs.

3. Set Healthy Boundaries

The nonstop news cycle can be exhausting, so protect your well-being:

- **Limit Consumption:** Dedicate specific times for catching up on news rather than allowing it to dominate your day.

- **Focus on Quality:** Prioritize stories that truly matter to you rather than chasing every headline.

- **Take Breaks:** Allow yourself to unplug when needed. Staying informed is a long-term commitment, not a one-time sprint.

4. Engage Thoughtfully

Using your toolkit isn't just about personal clarity—it's about contributing to a more informed society:

- **Challenge Misinformation:** Politely correct false claims in conversations or on social media, using credible sources to back up your points.

- **Share Reliable Content:** Amplify articles and stories from reputable outlets to help others access accurate information.

- **Start Discussions:** Use your insights to foster thoughtful conversations in your community.

5. Strengthen Your Confidence

The ultimate power of your toolkit lies in how it equips you to make informed decisions:

- **Build Understanding:** The more you engage with credible sources, the more nuanced your grasp of issues will become.

- **Take Action:** Use your knowledge to vote, advocate, or support causes that align with your values.

- **Trust Yourself:** Clarity breeds confidence. Trust that your thoughtful approach makes your voice a meaningful part of the democratic process.

6. Evaluate Your Toolkit Regularly

Your toolkit isn't static—it should grow and adapt:

- **Add New Sources:** As your interests evolve, include outlets that align with those topics.

- **Evaluate Trustworthiness:** Periodically review your sources to ensure they continue to meet your standards of accuracy and balance.

7. Be Part of the Solution

An informed citizenry is the backbone of a thriving democracy. By using your toolkit effectively, you:

- **Combat Misinformation:** Every time you verify a claim or share accurate information, you strengthen the culture of truth.

- **Promote Dialogue:** Engaged citizens foster meaningful discussions that drive progress.

- **Inspire Others:** Your example encourages friends, family, and community members to prioritize reliable information.

Final Thoughts

Your information toolkit is more than just a collection of sources—it's your anchor in the chaos, your guide to engaging confidently with the world. By using it intentionally, you amplify your voice and contribute to a healthier, more informed democracy.

The key is to stay curious and make the process enjoyable. You don't need to track every headline or untangle every narrative—that's a surefire way to burn out. Instead, focus on the stories that resonate with your passions and priorities. Whether it's climate change, local politics, healthcare, or education, let those interests guide your attention. Think of it like picking your favorite genre in the larger story of life.

Keeping your toolkit of reliable sources close allows you to stay informed without feeling overwhelmed. Take time to explore, question, and delve into the topics that matter most to you. Stay open to surprises—learning about issues outside your usual radar can be a rewarding adventure. The world is full of opportunities to expand your understanding, and a curious mindset keeps it exciting.

Remember, staying informed doesn't have to feel like a chore. It can be a way to connect with the wonder of a constantly evolving world. When you focus on what truly matters, stay grounded, and embrace a sense of exploration, you're not just a passive observer—you're an active participant in shaping the future.

And that's the magic of being an informed, engaged citizen: you're part of the biggest, most dynamic story there is. So grab your toolkit, follow your curiosity, and dive in. The next chapter is already unfolding, and you have the power to shape how the story continues.

How Change Begins

In 1971, a massive shift in public understanding occurred when The New York Times published the Pentagon Papers, a classified government report detailing decades of U.S. political and military involvement in Vietnam. Leaked by Daniel Ellsberg, a former military analyst, these documents revealed that successive administrations had systematically misled the public about the scope and success of the war.

For years, Americans had been fed a narrative of steady progress in Vietnam, while the truth was far more grim. The government had downplayed losses, exaggerated victories, and concealed growing doubts about the war's success. This misinformation led to a deepening conflict that cost countless lives and fractured the nation.

When the Pentagon Papers were published, they shattered the illusion. For the first time, many Americans had access to an unvarnished account of the decisions driving the war. This accurate, detailed information fueled widespread protests and significantly shifted public opinion, ultimately pressuring policymakers to rethink U.S. involvement.

The publication of the Pentagon Papers highlights the power of accurate information in helping people stay focused on what matters. Without access to the truth, the public was left in the dark, unable to make informed decisions about the war. With it, they could see clearly, ask the right questions, and hold their leaders accountable.

This story is a reminder that accurate sources of information are more than just tools—they're essential to navigating complex issues and staying focused on what truly matters. When we prioritize truth over spin and seek out reliable sources, we empower ourselves to see beyond the noise and act with clarity and purpose. The Pentagon Papers didn't just reveal the truth about Vietnam—they showed the enduring importance of informed citizens in shaping a better future.

Your Voice Matters

Wait! Don't skip! This isn't a pop-up ad trying to sell you fancy leggings or the world's fluffiest pillow. Nope, this is a shameless plea for something even more powerful: your review!

Thank you for joining me on this journey to empower voices and strengthen democracy. By now, you've seen how this book shines a light on the importance of civic engagement, critical thinking, and standing up for what matters. But did you know your voice can help amplify its impact?

It's quick and easy to do. Just scan the QR code, and you'll be taken straight to where you can share your review. Whether it's a few lines or a thoughtful reflection, your feedback matters.

Here's how: when you leave a review, you help others discover this book and its message. It's not just about me or the words I've written—it's about creating a movement. Your voice is vital in:

- **Building credibility.** Your perspective assures others that this book is worth their time and a valuable resource.

- **Boosting visibility.** Reviews are like a beacon, helping this book reach more people and make a bigger impact.

- **Inspiring action.** Your insights can ignite someone else's journey to becoming an active participant in democracy.

Together, we can create a ripple effect, inspiring more people to take a stand for democracy. Your voice is powerful—let it lead the way.

Thank you for being a part of this movement! High five for thinking about a review! Now let's dive back into the book and keep this democracy party rolling!

7

Navigating Misinformation—The Blessing and Curse of the Digital Age

Living in the digital age is remarkable, isn't it? You can binge an entire TV series on your phone, order pizza without uttering a word, or chat face-to-face with a friend halfway across the globe in mere seconds. Need to know the capital of Uzbekistan? Google delivers (it's Tashkent, by the way). The internet is an endless source of wonder, offering everything from the inner workings of an octopus's mind to the latest TikTok dance trends, 24/7.

But with all its perks comes a heavy catch. The same tools that bring us closer also create a breeding ground for misinformation. As we scroll through endless feeds or chase midnight rabbit holes, we're surrounded by bias, half-truths, and outright lies. It's a sea of noise, and knowing what's real feels increasingly like finding a needle in a haystack.

That's why it's so important to understand how misinformation works, why it's so pervasive, and how we can stay steady amidst the chaos. Because staying informed isn't just a personal win—it's a critical pillar of democracy itself

The internet has undeniably revolutionized how we engage with the world. A few clicks can reveal your representative's voting record or clarify what's on your ballot. Researching political issues has never been easier. But alongside this incredible accessibility comes a darker side: a flood of deliberate manipulation and out-right falsehoods designed to confuse, divide, and control.

Imagine stepping into the world's largest library, only to find some books mislabeled, others blatantly fictional, and some strategically crafted to mislead. It's overwhelming, and at times exhausting, to navigate. And the most alarming part? Misinformation doesn't just sprout from obscure corners of the web. It often originates from leaders—politicians, candidates, even elected officials—who wield immense power and influence.

So, why do leaders perpetuate misinformation? Sometimes it's about rallying support with emotionally charged narratives that push people to act without question. Other times, it's a strategic distraction—a way to deflect criticism or sow doubt about opponents. And often, it's about undermining trust, making the public so disoriented that consolidating power becomes easier.

This behavior isn't just frustrating; it's dangerous. Leaders are sup-posed to represent our interests, not manipulate us. Letting their falsehoods go unchecked isn't an option. It's like ignoring a friend's harmful behavior—you either call them out or set boundaries. Our leaders deserve the same accountability.

Pesky Trolls

Do Not Feed

The golden rule in social media: Don't feed the trolls. Trolls are digital agitators who thrive on stirring up conflict. Whether driven by boredom, a hidden agenda, or organized campaigns, trolls aim to provoke emotional reactions and amplify division. Their game? Visibility and chaos. Your best strategy? Don't engage. Block, report, and redirect your energy toward educating others and fostering meaningful dialogue. Trolls win when we play along, so the simplest solution is not to play at all.

Misinformation thrives on emotional manipulation. Fear, anger, and outrage are powerful drivers that can make us act impulsively or share unverified content. When something sparks your emotions, pause. Ask yourself: What's the intent here? Is it credible? Taking a moment to think critically disrupts misinformation's grip.

While this topic feels heavy, staying informed doesn't have to be a chore. The world is fascinating, messy, and brimming with surprises. Treat staying informed like solving a mystery. Curiosity can guide you to assemble pieces from reliable sources, painting a clearer picture of the bigger story.

The flood of misinformation might feel like an unstoppable storm, but don't let it push you into cynicism or apathy. Think of democracy as the ultimate group project. It takes all of us showing up, sifting through the noise, and refusing to back down. Every effort—every fact-checked article, every paused reaction—shapes the kind of democracy we all deserve.

Concluding Thoughts

Navigating the digital age can feel like walking a tightrope. The internet offers a wealth of information, entertainment, and connection, but it also demands vigilance against the pull of misinformation and emotional manipulation. The good news? You're not powerless in this dynamic. Far from it.

Every time you pause to question a headline, verify a claim, or choose not to share that sensational post, you're not just protecting yourself—you're fortifying democracy. Being informed is an act of care, not only for your own understanding but for the collective truth that holds our communities together. The ripple effect of thoughtful engagement is profound; it fosters trust, sharpens conversations, and paves the way for solutions grounded in reality.

It's easy to feel overwhelmed by the scale of the challenge or discouraged by the persistence of falsehoods. But remember this: meaningful change doesn't require perfection, only participation. By staying curious, asking the right questions, and committing to informed action, you're contributing to a culture that values truth and dialogue over division and distraction

Democracy isn't a spectator sport, and the digital chaos isn't a reason to sit on the sidelines. Instead, it's a call to step forward with clarity and purpose. Your voice, your choices, and your vigilance make a difference. Together, our collective efforts to seek truth and share knowledge can shape a brighter, more informed future.

So, let's keep showing up—not just for ourselves, but for each other. The path isn't always easy, but it's worth it. Because when we navigate the digital landscape with intention and care, we're not just participating in democracy—we're building it, one thoughtful act at a time.

How Change Begins

On a quiet Sunday evening, October 30, 1938, Americans across the country tuned in to their radios for the usual evening programs. Remember, radios were the new technology of the time. This novel contraption made news and entertainment immediately available in many homes for the first time in human history. But instead of orchestras or variety shows, this day they were met with a chilling bulletin: explosions on Mars and reports of strange cylindrical objects landing in New Jersey. A frantic announcer described chaos as towering alien machines emerged, destroying everything in their path.

What listeners didn't realize—at least not right away—was that this was a fictional radio play: Orson Welles' adaptation of H.G. Wells' The War of the Worlds. Presented in the format of breaking news, it was so realistic that many believed it was happening in real time.

Panic spread. Families fled their homes, traffic jams clogged roads, and terrified listeners called police stations to report alien sightings. One man in New Jersey wrapped his house in wet blankets to protect it from the alien's "heat ray." The nation's trust in radio, then a dominant source of news, turned this theatrical experiment into a full-blown crisis of misinformation.

When the truth emerged the next day, the nation was shaken—not by Martians, but by how easily misinformation had taken hold. The broadcast revealed a stark reality: in a rapidly modernizing world, where mass communication moved faster than fact-checking, misinformation had the power to manipulate emotions and derail reason.

But here's where change began. In the aftermath, Americans started asking hard questions: How do we trust what we hear? How can media responsibly present information? And what's our responsibility as listeners to question what's presented to us? The Federal Communications Commission (FCC) stepped up efforts to regulate broadcasts, setting guidelines to prevent future chaos. Educators began emphasizing media literacy, planting the seeds of critical thinking in classrooms nationwide.

The War of the Worlds panic became more than a moment of collective fear—it became a turning point. It reminded the nation that change doesn't come from avoiding mistakes but from recognizing them and doing better. Awareness of the power of information—and the responsibility to question it—was the first step in a larger cultural shift toward media accountability and public skepticism.

Even today, the lesson resonates. In a world flooded with instant news and social media, the need to pause, verify, and think critically is more important than ever. Just as the panic of 1938 forced Americans to rethink how they consume information, every misstep offers the chance to grow. Because change begins when we confront the chaos, learn from it, and choose to move forward with clarity and intention.

8

Democracy Doesn't Start or Stop on Election Day

L et's be honest—when you hear "showing up for democracy," your mind probably jumps to Election Day. Maybe you picture waiting in line at the polls, filling out a mail-in ballot, or proudly wearing that "I Voted" sticker. It's the big event, democracy's version of the Super Bowl. But here's the truth: democracy is so much more than one day every few years. It's alive, ongoing, and built on the moments in between. Showing up for democracy doesn't start and stop with casting your vote—it's a way of living, a mindset, and an invitation to make a difference every day.

How many times have you seen or heard about an issue and thought, I hope someone does something about that? That thought isn't just a fleeting wish—it's your passion trying to get your attention. It's a spark, calling you to act. And while it might feel like someone else's responsibility, maybe, just maybe, it's your opportunity, your moment, your chance to create change.

Democracy lives in the everyday. It's in the choices made about your neighborhood park, the resources allocated to your local schools, and the policies that affect healthcare, housing, and public safety. It's in the conversations you have, the values you share, and the community you help shape. Democracy isn't just about big, headline-grabbing actions—it's about showing up in the small, consistent ways that ripple outward and build momentum for change.

When you show up for your community, you're showing up for democracy. Volunteering at a local food bank, attending a PTA meeting, advocating for a new crosswalk in your neighborhood, or organizing a book drive are all democratic acts. These moments—often dismissed as "just community service" or "someone else's job"—are the foundation of a healthy democracy. When we work to make our communities better, we are practicing democracy at its most essential level: people coming together to improve the places where we live, learn, and grow.

Year-round involvement doesn't have to mean adding more to your to-do list—it's about recognizing how your existing actions already contribute and finding ways to deepen your engagement. The next time you notice a problem or feel drawn to an issue, take a moment to reflect: What can I do here? It doesn't have to be big. It could be as simple as starting a conversation, signing a petition, joining a community cleanup, or sharing information with friends. These small steps create ripples, and those ripples can turn into waves.

But democracy is not a solo endeavor—it thrives on connection. Collaboration makes our efforts more meaningful and impactful. When you talk to neighbors about shared concerns, join a local group working on a project, or team up with others to address a challenge, you're strengthening the fabric of democracy. It's in these shared efforts, big and small, that we find our collective power.

Feeling overwhelmed by where to start? Start with what moves you. Pay attention to the moments when you think, I wish someone would do something. That's your passion pointing you toward action. If you care about education, attend a school board meeting or volunteer to tutor kids in your neighborhood. If you're passionate about the environment, join a local park cleanup or write to your representative about climate policy. Whatever your interest, there's a way to act on it—and it doesn't have to be perfect. What matters is showing up.

The beauty of democracy is that it's adaptable and flexible. It doesn't demand grand gestures; it calls for steady, thoughtful participation. Every person's role looks different, and that's its strength. Some will march in the streets, while others will write letters or make phone calls. Some will lead initiatives, while others will provide quiet support behind the scenes. Each contribution is valuable. Each action builds the whole.

Engaging in democracy year-round isn't just about strengthening your community—it's about strengthening yourself. It gives you a sense of purpose, turning frustration into action and helplessness into empowerment. That thought—I hope someone does something about that—is your invitation to be that someone. Every time you act, you affirm that your voice and choices matter, not just for you, but for your neighbors, your family, and future generations.

Democracy is alive, and it thrives when we embrace it as a shared responsibility. It's not about waiting for the "right time" or the "right person" to come along—it's about recognizing that the time is now, and the person is you. Every conversation, every action, every step forward strengthens the collective effort that keeps democracy vibrant.

So, take a breath and start where you are. Find an issue that lights a fire in you. Connect with others who care. Take one small step, and then another. Show up in a way that feels right for you. Whether it's joining a campaign, advocating for a cause, or simply helping a neighbor, your actions matter. They all add up to something bigger—a democracy that reflects the best of who we are and what we care about.

Together, we create a democracy that doesn't just survive, but thrives. One that isn't confined to Election Day but lives in the spaces where we show up, work together, and make things better. The first step is yours to take. Let's take it, together.

Concluding Thoughts

Democracy is alive, and it thrives when we embrace it as a shared responsibility. It's not about waiting for the "right time" or the "right person" to come along—it's about recognizing that the time is now, and the person is you. Every conversation, every action, every step forward strengthens the collective effort that keeps democracy vibrant.

So, take a breath and start where you are. Find an issue that lights a fire in you. Connect with others who care. Take one small step, and then another. Show up in a way that feels right for you. Whether it's joining a campaign, advocating for a cause, or simply helping a neighbor, your actions matter. They all add up to something bigger—a democracy that reflects the best of who we are and what we care about.

Together, we create a democracy that doesn't just survive, but thrives. One that isn't confined to Election Day but lives in the spaces where we show up, work together, and make things better. The first step is yours to take. Let's take it, together.

How Change Begins

Opal Lee was 89 years old when she decided to take the first step—literally. Wearing her sturdy sneakers and a wide-brimmed hat, she set out on a journey she hoped would spark a conversation across the nation. Her goal? To make Juneteenth, the day commemorating the end of slavery in the United States, a federal holiday.

Starting in Fort Worth, Texas, Opal walked two and a half miles—a symbolic nod to the two and a half years it took for enslaved people in Texas to learn they were free after the Emancipation Proclamation. She didn't stop there. Town by town, she walked, talked, and shared her vision with anyone who would listen. Some days, it was a crowd; other days, just one or two curious people. But Opal believed in the ripple effect of change—how one conversation could inspire another, and another, until it became unstoppable.

People began to notice. Local leaders joined her, then national ones. What started as an idea in one woman's heart spread like wildfire. By 2021, after decades of effort, her dream became a reality. President Biden signed the Juneteenth National Independence Day Act into law, and Opal Lee stood at the White House, a testament to the power of persistence and small steps.

Opal's story is a reminder that change doesn't begin with sweeping gestures—it begins with showing up. One walk. One conversation. One moment of courage. Her journey proves that no matter your age or resources, you can be the spark that lights the way forward.

So, as you think about how democracy fits into your life, remember Opal Lee. Change starts with one step, one voice, one action. And just like Opal, you never know how far it can go.

9

Democracy is a Team Sport

Democracy isn't just a system of government; it's a team sport built on collaboration, shared goals, and collective action. At its best, democracy thrives when everyone brings their unique strengths to the game, working together to overcome challenges, celebrate victories, and keep the momentum going. It's not about politics alone—it's about people, connection, and the courage to show up for each other.

Playing the Game Together

Imagine democracy as a team sport. On your own, you might shoot a few baskets or run drills, but the magic of the game comes when the team takes the court. Each player brings something unique—some excel at defense, others lead the offense, and still others rally the team with their energy. Together, these individual contributions create a dynamic, winning strategy.

Democracy works the same way. It relies on the diverse skills, perspectives, and passions of its players to succeed. Every vote, every conversation, and every small action is like a pass, a shot, or an assist. And just like in sports, no one wins alone. Collaboration is what turns individual effort into collective progress.

But just like a team sport, democracy requires practice and care. Neglect it, and it falters—misinformation, apathy, and division can steal the ball. Yet when we show up, ready to play, debate ideas, and find common ground, democracy becomes stronger, more resilient, and capable of creating a brighter future.

Embracing Differences: The Key to a Strong Team

A winning team isn't made up of identical players—it thrives on diversity. Each player's unique skills and perspectives contribute to the team's success. Similarly, democracy thrives when we embrace differences as a strength. Healthy disagreement is the foundation of progress, helping us see the full court, identify blind spots, and create better solutions.

Of course, disagreements can sometimes feel like fouls in the game—disruptive and frustrating. The key is to approach them with respect and strategy, keeping the focus on collaboration rather than conflict.

Here's how to navigate disagreements like a pro:

- **Assume Good Intention:** Trust that your teammates—whether in conversation or action—are aiming for the same goal, even if their approach differs. This mindset builds trust and fosters mutual respect.

- **Seek to Understand:** Ask questions to understand the other person's perspective. What drives their ideas? Finding common ground strengthens teamwork.

- **Separate Ideas from Identity:** Remember, challenging someone's idea isn't rejecting them as a person. Focus on the play, not the player.

- **Stay Fact-Focused:** Ground your discussion in shared realities. Facts are like the rulebook, keeping the game fair and productive.

- **Respond, Don't React:** Take a moment before replying. A measured response keeps emotions in check and prevents escalation.

- **Acknowledge Valid Points:** Recognizing the strengths in someone else's argument builds trust and shows you value their input.

- **Agree to Disagree:** Not every play will end in agreement, and that's okay. The game continues, and every contribution moves the team forward.

Handling Aggression and Conflict

In every game, there are moments when tensions run high, and the competition feels heated. When faced with aggression or hostility, the goal is to keep your composure and stay focused on the bigger picture. Here's how to handle those situations:

- **Stay Calm and Focused:** When faced with aggression, respond like a skilled player under pressure—steady and composed. Lower your voice, take a breath, and don't let the heat of the moment derail you.

- **Set Boundaries:** If a conversation becomes hostile, call a timeout. Calmly state, "I'm happy to continue this discussion, but we need to keep it respectful."

- **De-escalate with Empathy:** Acknowledge the emotions at play without engaging in the aggression: "I can tell this matters deeply to you."

- **Avoid Matching Aggression:** Aggression feeds on aggression. Instead, use neutral language to redirect the focus to the issue at hand.

- **Know When to Walk Away:** Sometimes, the best move is to step off the court. Disengage politely, and don't feel obligated to continue in an unproductive or unsafe environment.

- **Reflect and Regroup:** After a heated interaction, take time to process what happened and think about how you might handle similar situations in the future. Practice self-care and heal your emotions. Releasing the moment helps your mind and body from developing a trigger that impacts your future engagements. Let a tough moment just be a moment.

When you handle conflict with grace and resolve, you keep the team's focus on the goal and set the tone for future collaboration.

Finding Your Team

No great game is ever won alone. Democracy is a team sport, and the power of collective action cannot be overstated. Start by finding your teammates—people who share your values, your vision, or your passion for change.

Begin small. Maybe it's a friend who shares your concerns about local issues or a coworker who's passionate about a cause. These initial connections are like passing the ball; they build momentum. Attend town halls, join advocacy groups, or connect with like-minded people online. Look for spaces that welcome diverse perspectives and focus on actionable solutions. If something doesn't feel like a good fit, move on—there's a team for everyone.

Democracy as a Collective Force

When a team works together, they're unstoppable. History reminds us of this truth. From civil rights marches to grassroots movements, every major victory was built on the collective effort of people willing to show up, work together, and play their role.

Your contribution doesn't need to be dramatic. Every action, no matter how small, matters. Whether you're writing letters, organizing events, or simply showing up to vote, you're helping the team move forward. Democracy thrives because of diverse contributions.

Here's the secret: democracy doesn't have to feel like a chore—it can be inspiring, energizing, and even fun. Make it social—celebrate Election Day with friends, host conversations over snacks, or cheer each other on as you tackle issues together. Bring creativity to the game—design posters, share uplifting messages, or create memes that spread awareness. When you make democracy personal and joyful, you're more likely to stay engaged.

Celebrate the wins—big and small. Whether your candidate succeeds, a policy you care about passes, or you simply make it to the polls after a busy day, take a moment to recognize your effort. Every step forward is worth acknowledging.

Concluding Thoughts

Democracy isn't just about showing up—it's about playing the game together. Like any great team, we rely on each other's strengths, resilience, and shared commitment to the goal. By embracing differences, managing conflict with grace, and showing up for the collective good, we ensure democracy remains vibrant and strong.

Your voice is powerful. Your actions matter. Step onto the court—whether in conversation, collaboration, or quiet contribution—and know that you're part of a team that's shaping the future. Together, we play for progress, justice, and a brighter tomorrow.

Let's keep the ball moving. Let's play to win.

How Change Begins

In 1838, a young Frederick Douglass escaped slavery, risking his life for the chance to live as a free man. But freedom didn't feel like the victory he'd imagined. In the North, he was still surrounded by prejudice, inequality, and a system that denied the humanity of people like him. Alone in a new world, Douglass knew he wanted to fight for change—but he couldn't do it alone.

His turning point came in 1841, when he attended an abolitionist meeting in Nantucket. He wasn't a planned speaker, but when he stood to share his story, the room was electrified. Among those moved by his words was William Lloyd Garrison, the fiery editor of The Liberator, a leading abolitionist newspaper. Garrison saw not just Douglass's pain, but his power.

The two men formed a bond that would alter the course of history. Garrison invited Douglass to join the abolitionist movement, and for the first time, Douglass found himself surrounded by people who shared his vision of a country free from the shackles of slavery. This community became Douglass's tribe, giving him the platform, resources, and camaraderie he needed to amplify his voice.

With his tribe behind him, Douglass published his first autobiography, Narrative of the Life of Frederick Douglass, an American Slave, which exposed the horrors of slavery to audiences across the globe. He became a sought-after speaker and one of the most influential abolitionists of his time.

Douglass's story shows that even the most extraordinary individuals need a team. By finding his tribe—people who believed in his mission and helped him amplify his voice—Douglass turned personal pain into collective action. Together, they helped ignite a movement that would change the nation forever.

Because, as Douglass himself once said, "If there is no struggle, there is no progress." And finding the right people to struggle alongside can make all the difference.

10

Grassroots Movements: Growing Change from the Ground Up

G rassroots is a term we hear often in conversations about activism, politics, and social change. But what does it truly mean? For many, it evokes images of marches and rallies, but the essence of grassroots movements lies far deeper. At their core, these movements are about ordinary people—neighbors, coworkers, families—uniting to confront challenges in their communities. They are bottom-up efforts, driven by the belief that those closest to a problem are best equipped to find solutions.

Unlike strategies crafted in distant boardrooms, grassroots movements grow from lived experiences. They start small—a conversation at a kitchen table, a text thread, or a library meeting—and can expand into powerful forces for change. They remind us that transformation often begins with a single step, taken by someone who dares to act.

Why Grassroots Movements Matter

The term "grassroots" is fitting. Like the roots of grass, these movements are decentralized, resilient, and interconnected. They emerge quietly but gain strength through collective energy. Each individual action—whether organizing a cleanup, starting a petition, or speaking at a community meeting—builds momentum and weaves a network of shared purpose.

What sets grassroots efforts apart is their authenticity. Unlike top-down solutions, which often feel detached, grassroots movements are rooted in personal stories and firsthand experiences. This genuine connection fosters trust, mobilizes communities, and inspires action. By working collaboratively, ordinary people take ownership of their future, ensuring that every voice matters.

Throughout history, grassroots movements have reshaped society. The Civil Rights Movement began in local churches and homes, with individuals like John Lewis and groups like the Student Nonviolent Coordinating Committee driving a nationwide demand for justice. More recently, the Fight for $15 started with a small group of fast-food workers advocating for fair wages, sparking a national conversation and legislative action focused on the minimum wage.

In times of crisis, grassroots organizers often step up where institutions fail. After Hurricane Katrina, local groups provided critical food, shelter, and medical care, proving that communities can rise to meet even the direst challenges. These stories underscore a vital truth: meaningful change doesn't always start with leaders or legislation—it begins with people like you.

The Heartbeat of Democracy

Grassroots movements embody democracy at its most vibrant. They remind us that democracy thrives when everyone takes part, not by waiting for others to lead but by stepping forward together.

Whether advocating for safer streets, cleaner air, or economic fairness, these movements prove that small, persistent actions can drive monumental change.

Participation in a grassroots movement doesn't require expertise or titles—just a willingness to care and connect. When individuals unite around shared concerns, their collective voice becomes powerful enough to shift policies, challenge inequities, and transform perceptions.

These movements also teach us the power of persistence. Change rarely happens overnight; it is the culmination of countless small actions sustained over time. Grassroots efforts demonstrate that progress is possible even when the path is slow or filled with obstacles.

The metaphor of grass is also apt because no single blade can cover a field, but together, they form a vast, interconnected landscape. Similarly, when individuals act collectively, their impact far exceeds what any one person could achieve alone. Grassroots movements remind us that democracy is strongest when built from the ground up.

Concluding Thoughts

At their best, grassroots movements amplify marginalized voices, challenge apathy, and demand accountability. They thrive on authenticity and human connection, offering a powerful antidote to cynicism and disconnection. These movements teach us that real power lies not in institutions but in people who care deeply and act boldly.

As we reflect on the stories of grassroots organizing—past and present—we see a common thread: their success depends on individuals willing to show up, speak out, and work together. Every letter written, every meeting held, and every action taken plants a seed for future growth.

Grassroots movements are not just about addressing immediate problems; they are about building stronger, more connected communities. They remind us that change starts with us—not as bystanders, but as active participants in shaping a better future. When we choose to engage, we don't just advocate for change; we create it.

Real change begins with ordinary people stepping into their extraordinary potential. The question is not whether one person can make a difference but how we can collectively amplify that difference to transform the world.

How Change Begins

In 2013, Alicia Garza sat down to write a Facebook post after hearing that George Zimmerman had been acquitted in the killing of Trayvon Martin. Filled with grief and frustration, she penned a heartfelt message, concluding with three words: "Black lives matter." Her friend Patrisse Cullors shared the post, adding a hashtag, and Opal Tometi built a digital platform to amplify the phrase. What began as an expression of anguish quickly grew into something larger—a rallying cry that resonated across the country.

The phrase "Black Lives Matter" gained momentum online, but its true power emerged in the streets. In Ferguson, Missouri, the killing of Michael Brown in 2014 sparked massive protests. People from all over gathered to demand justice and an end to police brutality. There was no central leader directing the movement—it was driven by neighbors, friends, and local activists, each contributing their voice and energy. It was raw, personal, and deeply rooted in the lived experiences of those affected.

By 2020, Black Lives Matter had grown into a global movement. The murder of George Floyd ignited protests around the world, with millions marching to demand change. Communities organized food drives, medical aid, and healing spaces alongside their calls for justice. In Washington, D.C., activists worked with city leaders to paint the words "Black Lives Matter" in giant yellow letters across a two-block stretch of 16th Street, just steps from the White House. The street became a powerful symbol of the movement, a visual declaration that could not be ignored.

The power of Black Lives Matter lies in its grassroots origins. It began with a simple statement of truth and grew through the collective action of people united by a shared purpose. The movement reminds us that real change starts with those closest to the problem and that the voices of ordinary people can echo far beyond their communities. What started as a hashtag became a global force, proving that even the smallest spark can ignite a revolution.

11

Finding Joy in Showing Up

Let's face it—when someone mentions "democratic engage-ment," your first thought probably isn't, "This will change my life!" Instead, you might picture dry meetings, heated arguments, or long lines at the polls. But what if democracy could be something more—something meaningful, energizing, and deeply connected to your sense of self?

Here's the thing: democracy doesn't have to feel like a chore. At its best, it's not just a system of government—it's a mirror that reflects who you are and what you value. When you show up, you're not only contributing to the world; you're also giving something back to yourself. Research shows that engaging in meaningful action activates the brain's reward system, releasing dopamine, which fuels motivation and enhances feelings of accomplishment. It's why taking action—even small steps—feels so deeply satisfying.[1]

Living with a sense of purpose has profound benefits for your well-being. A landmark study in The Lancet found that people who align their actions with their values experience improved mental health, greater resilience, and even longer lives. The study emphasized that purpose-driven individuals are better equipped to handle stress and are more likely to thrive, regardless of life's challenges,[2] When you align your energy with causes that matter, you're not just addressing the world's problems—you're tapping into a wellspring of personal strength and fulfillment.

Consider the story of a group of high school students in Stockton, California, who started a small community garden to combat local food insecurity. What began as a simple idea—turning an empty lot into a space for fresh produce—quickly became a source of transformation. These students didn't just grow vegetables; they grew a stronger sense of self-worth and connection to their community. Many reported feeling more hopeful and confident because they were directly addressing a problem they cared about. The ripple effect of their efforts extended beyond the garden, inspiring others to get involved and sparking broader conversations about equity and access to healthy food. Their story reminds us that small, grassroots efforts can lead to profound personal and collective growth,[3]

The benefits of civic engagement go beyond a sense of purpose. Engaging in democracy connects you to others, creating a sense of belonging that is fundamental to human happiness. Greta Thunberg's climate activism is a powerful example. What began as a solitary school strike turned into a global movement that brought millions together, united by a shared vision of environmental action. Greta herself has said that activism gave her a sense of connection and hope—proof that showing up for a cause can counter feelings of isolation and despair.[4]

Even setbacks can take on new meaning when you're acting with purpose. Angela Duckworth's research on grit—the combination of passion and perseverance—shows that people who pursue meaningful goals are more resilient in the face of challenges. They see obstacles not as roadblocks but as stepping stones on the path to progress,[5] This perspective transforms how we experience struggles: rather than feeling stuck, we feel propelled forward by a sense of purpose.

The story of Malala Yousafzai illustrates this resilience. After surviving an attack on her life, Malala became a global advocate for girls' education, channeling personal trauma into a mission that changed the lives of millions. Her activism brought her hope, community, and a renewed sense of purpose. She often reflects on how speaking out gave her strength, proving that when you engage with the world, it not only amplifies your voice—it also strengthens your spirit.[6]

Democracy, at its core, is an invitation to connect—with your community, your values, and your potential. When you show up—whether to vote, rally, or write a letter—you're engaging in an act of self-expression that says, "I matter. My voice matters." This act of claiming your space in the world is transformative. It builds confidence, sharpens your sense of identity, and reminds you that you're part of something bigger.

This isn't about perfection. It's about taking one step and seeing where it leads. When you show up, you'll find that the impact isn't just on the world around you—it's on your own sense of fulfillment. You'll feel more joyful, capable, more connected, and more alive.

So here's the truth: showing up changes lives—starting with your own. It's not just an obligation or a duty. It's an opportunity to feel the thrill of contributing to something meaningful, to experience the joy of connection, and to discover your own power. Democracy is the ultimate mirror, reflecting not only the world we live in but also the person we're becoming. And when you show up, you're proving to yourself—and the world—that you matter.

Concluding Thoughts

Democracy gives back what we put into it—our energy, our ideas, our values. When you approach it with passion and purpose, it doesn't just transform the system. It transforms you. You become more engaged, more connected, and more fulfilled.

So let this be your invitation: find the issues that light you up, lean into them, and let them guide you. Because when you show up not out of obligation but out of passion, you're not just participating in democracy—you're making it your own. And that's where real, lasting change begins.

How Change Begins

In the early 2000s, the fight for marriage equality in the United States faced an uphill battle. Public opinion was split, many politicians were hesitant to support the cause, and legal barriers seemed insurmountable. But instead of relying solely on traditional activism, a group of advocates decided to take a different, more personal approach: telling stories.

The Freedom to Marry campaign, led by Evan Wolfson and a coalition of activists, wasn't just about changing laws—it was about changing hearts. They realized that one of the most powerful tools for shifting public opinion wasn't stats or legal jargon; it was authenticity. The campaign focused on storytelling, using real-life examples of love, commitment, and family to make the case for equality.

Couples shared their stories on TV ads, social media, and at community events, showing the world that their love was no different from anyone else's. Parents of LGBTQ+ children spoke out, framing the issue not as abstract politics but as a deeply personal matter of fairness and dignity. These stories weren't flashy or confrontational—they were raw, relatable, and deeply human.

At the same time, the campaign creatively targeted local communities. Instead of focusing only on national debates, they worked at the state level, building grassroots movements to push for change one step at a time. From house parties to pride parades to heartfelt letters to the editor, the message was clear: marriage equality wasn't just a policy—it was about people's lives.

By the time the Supreme Court legalized same-sex marriage nationwide in 2015, public opinion had shifted dramatically. What was once a divisive issue had gained majority support, thanks in large part to the power of authenticity and connection.

The Freedom to Marry campaign is a testament to the idea that change doesn't always come from loud protests or flashy stunts. Sometimes, it comes from being real—sharing your story, listening to others, and finding the common ground that reminds us all of our shared humanity.

12

Finding Your Passion

Passion isn't something that simply arrives one day like a package on your doorstep. It's something you discover—piece by piece—through curiosity, exploration, and reflection. Think of it as a journey, a path you carve with each step you take toward what excites and fulfills you. This chapter isn't just about finding your passion. It's about helping you embrace the process, recognizing that the journey itself can be just as meaningful as the destination.

Let's begin with a moment. Think back to a time when you felt deeply connected to something you were doing. Maybe you were helping a friend through a tough situation, planting a garden, or speaking up about something that mattered to you. Recall how it felt—how time seemed to fade away as your focus sharpened and your energy grew. That's the feeling we're aiming for: the sensation of being so aligned with your actions that they become an extension of who you are.

The good news? That feeling isn't reserved for rare moments. It's something you can cultivate by exploring what matters most to you.

Following the Clues

Passion often starts with curiosity—a spark that lights up your mind and whispers, Pay attention. It might be a story that lingers in your thoughts, a problem that frustrates you, or a moment that makes your heart race. These are the breadcrumbs leading you toward what resonates.

Take Lena, for example. She had always loved spending time outdoors but didn't think of herself as an "activist." One day, while hiking her favorite trail, she noticed how litter and erosion were changing the landscape she loved. It wasn't a dramatic moment—just a quiet realization that stirred something in her. She began volunteering for local clean-up efforts and eventually joined a committee focused on conservation. Along the way, Lena discovered not only her passion for protecting natural spaces but also a community of like-minded people who shared her values. What started as a simple observation grew into a purpose that gave her life new direction.

Like Lena, you don't have to know exactly where you're headed. Start by paying attention to the moments that make you pause. Ask yourself:

- What stories catch my attention and stay with me?

- When do I feel most alive, energized, or deeply moved?

- What problems or issues make me think, Someone should do something about this?

These moments aren't random. They're clues. Follow them.

Reflecting on Your Values

Passion doesn't exist in isolation—it's rooted in your values. These are the principles that guide you, the compass that points you toward what feels meaningful. Reflecting on your values helps you uncover the causes and actions that align with your deepest beliefs.

Think of Raj, a teacher who always emphasized fairness in his classroom. Over time, he realized this value extended far beyond his work—he was deeply troubled by disparities in education, especially for underfunded schools in his district. When a local coalition began advocating for more equitable funding, Raj joined without hesitation. His passion wasn't born from something new; it was the natural extension of values he'd held all along.

Your values are like seeds, waiting for the right soil to grow. Ask yourself:

- What do I believe in so strongly that I feel compelled to act?

- What principles guide my decisions, even in small ways?

- How have my experiences shaped what I care about most?

Sometimes, your values are hidden in plain sight. Look closely, and you'll find them.

Listening to Your Emotions

Passion isn't always logical—it's emotional. It's the fire in your gut when you see an injustice or the quiet joy you feel when you're immersed in something you love. Emotions are powerful indicators of where your passions lie.

Consider Jamie, who always found herself brimming with excitement during neighborhood block parties. She loved the connections, the laughter, and the sense of belonging that grew from these gatherings. Over time, she realized she wanted to bring that same sense of community to other spaces. She started organizing events at the local library, fostering connections among neighbors who might not otherwise meet. Her passion for building community wasn't something she planned—it was something she felt.

Your emotions are your guide. Pay attention to moments of joy, anger, or frustration. They often point to where your energy wants to flow.

Experimenting with Curiosity

You don't need to have everything figured out to start. Passion often reveals itself through action. Testing the waters—trying new things without pressure—can lead to surprising discoveries.

Anna always admired activists but never saw herself as one. When a friend invited her to a rally for voting rights, she hesitated but decided to go. She found herself moved by the speeches and energized by the crowd. From there, she volunteered to help register voters, realizing how much she enjoyed empowering others. Today, Anna organizes workshops on voter education, all because she took one small step into the unknown.

What might you discover by trying something new? Volunteer for an afternoon. Join a local meeting. Talk to a friend about an issue they care about. Each action, no matter how small, is a step forward.

Embracing the Process

Here's the truth: finding your passion is a journey, not a destination. It's an evolving process that grows as you grow. What excites you today might change tomorrow, and that's okay. The key is to stay open—to keep following the threads of curiosity, values, and emotions that guide you.

Think of your passion as a garden. It needs time, care, and patience to flourish. There will be moments of uncertainty, but each step brings you closer to understanding what matters most. Along the way, you'll discover not just what you care about but also the strength and resilience within yourself.

A List for Inspiration

If you're wondering where to begin, let this list of topics inspire you . As you reflect on these ideas, ask yourself: What makes me feel excited, hopeful, or motivated?

Your passion might not be on this list, and that's okay. Use it as a starting point to discover what resonates with you. Finding your passion is about discovering what feels meaningful to you. Once you find that spark, the rest will follow. Your journey starts here. Let your curiosity guide you.

1. Affordable Housing

- What It Is: Fighting to make homes affordable for everyone and ending homelessness.

- Why It Matters: Rent is skyrocketing, and young people are being priced out of cities where they dream of living and working. Your generation deserves secure, affordable places to call home.

2. AI and Job Automation

- What It Is: Ensuring AI doesn't replace jobs without creating new opportunities.

- Why It Matters: Automation is changing everything. If we don't act, people—especially younger workers—could be left behind. But with smart policies, AI can enhance careers, not destroy them.

3. Artificial Intelligence Regulation

- What It Is: Keeping AI ethical and fair, and stopping it from being misused.

- Why It Matters: AI impacts everything from what you see on social media to hiring decisions. Without regulation, it could reinforce bias, invade privacy, or even threaten democracy.

4. Anti-Corruption Measures

- What It Is: Holding leaders accountable and stopping corruption.

- Why It Matters: Corruption steals resources from things that matter—education, healthcare, and your future. Imagine a world where leaders actually work for you.

5. Child Welfare

- What It Is: Making sure kids have food, safety, and opportunities to thrive.

- Why It Matters: Kids are the future, and if they're neglected, society suffers. Fighting for their well-being means a better world for everyone.

6. Climate Change and Environmental Policy

- What It Is: Stopping climate destruction by cutting emissions and protecting the planet.

- Why It Matters: This is your future. Rising temperatures, wildfires, and extreme weather are already here. Take action now, and you'll help ensure a livable planet for generations to come.

7. Climate Justice

- **What It Is:** Making sure climate solutions include everyone, especially marginalized groups.

- **Why It Matters:** Communities that didn't cause the problem are paying the highest price. Fighting for climate justice means fairness and equality in tackling the biggest issue of our time.

8. Corporate Accountability

- **What It Is:** Holding big businesses responsible for fair practices and paying their share.

- **Why It Matters:** Corporations control so much of the world's wealth. Pushing them to act ethically means a fairer, more balanced system.

9. Criminal Justice Reform

- **What It Is:** Ending mass incarceration, reforming policing, and ensuring fairness.

- **Why It Matters:** The justice system disproportionately harms communities of color and the poor. Reform is about creating equality and safety for everyone.

10. Cybersecurity

- **What It Is:** Protecting your data and digital systems from cyberattacks.

- **Why It Matters:** Our lives are online. If systems fail or data is stolen, it affects your safety, identity, and future opportunities.

11. Digital Privacy and Data Protection

- What It Is: Making sure your personal information stays private.

- Why It Matters: Companies profit off your data without your permission. Take back control over who knows what about you.

12. Disability Rights and Inclusion

- What It Is: Creating a world that works for everyone, regardless of ability.

- Why It Matters: Accessibility isn't a bonus; it's a right. A more inclusive society means innovation, fairness, and empowerment.

13. Economic Inequality

- What It Is: Narrowing the wealth gap between the ultra-rich and the rest of us.

- Why It Matters: The current system rewards the wealthy and leaves the rest struggling. By fighting inequality, you're fighting for opportunity for all.

14. Education Equity

- What It Is: Giving every student access to great teachers, schools, and resources.

- Why It Matters: Your zip code shouldn't decide your future. Education equity means everyone gets a fair shot.

15. Food Security and Sustainable Agriculture

- What It Is: Ensuring people have enough to eat while protecting the planet.

- Why It Matters: Hunger is solvable. Sustainable farming practices ensure a future where everyone eats without destroying the Earth.

16. Foreign Policy

- What It Is: Creating peaceful, cooperative relationships with other countries.

- Why It Matters: Global issues—like climate change and health crises—need global solutions. Your voice matters in shaping how we engage with the world.

17. Freedom of Press and Media Accountability

- What It Is: Protecting journalism while fighting misinformation.

- Why It Matters: Without a free press, truth suffers. In the age of fake news, fighting for honest reporting has never been more important.

18. Gun Control and Safety

- What It Is: Implementing common-sense laws to reduce gun violence.

- Why It Matters: Gun violence is the leading cause of death for young people in the U.S. Your generation can demand change to save lives.

19. Healthcare Access for Marginalized Communities

- What It Is: Ensuring everyone gets the care they need, regardless of race or income.

- Why It Matters: Health disparities kill people. Fighting for equitable care saves lives and strengthens communities.

20. Healthcare Reform

- What It Is: Making healthcare affordable and accessible for everyone.

- Why It Matters: Medical bills are the #1 cause of bankruptcy. Reforming the system means saving lives and reducing stress.

21. Housing Affordability

- What It Is: Tackling rising rents and ensuring everyone has a safe place to live.

- Why It Matters: The dream of living independently shouldn't feel impossible. Affordable housing gives young people the freedom to pursue their goals.

22. Immigration and Border Policy

- What It Is: Creating humane pathways to citizenship and addressing border challenges.

- Why It Matters: Immigration builds diversity and innovation. By advocating for fair policies, you're helping create a more inclusive future.

23. Infrastructure Modernization

- What It Is: Revamping roads, public transit, broadband, and renewable energy grids.

- Why It Matters: Outdated infrastructure holds us back. Modernizing these systems improves daily life and builds sustainable cities for your future.

24. International Human Rights

- What It Is: Fighting for fairness, freedom, and dignity

worldwide.

- Why It Matters: When human rights are under attack any-where, it affects us all. Your voice can help hold oppressors accountable and inspire global change.

25. Internet Access and Net Neutrality

- What It Is: Expanding affordable internet and ensuring online freedoms.

- Why It Matters: The internet is essential for education, work, and connecting with the world. Protecting access ensures opportunity for everyone.

26. LGBTQ+ Rights

- What It Is: Defending the right to love, live, and express freely.

- Why It Matters: Discrimination against LGBTQ+ communi-ties is far from over. Your activism ensures equality and inclusion for all.

27. Mental Health Services

- What It Is: Improving access to mental health care and ending stigma.

- Why It Matters: Mental health matters just as much as physical health. Advocating for better services helps your friends, your family, and you.

28. Military and Defense Spending

- What It Is: Balancing spending on defense with invest-ments in education, healthcare, and innovation.

- Why It Matters: Spending billions on the military while neglecting urgent needs like housing and healthcare doesn't add up. Your advocacy can help rebalance priorities.

29. Pandemic Preparedness and Response

- What It Is: Strengthening health systems to handle future crises.

- Why It Matters: The pandemic changed everything. Ensuring we're ready for the next one protects lives and jobs.

30. Paid Family Leave

- What It Is: Guaranteeing time off to care for loved ones without losing income.

- Why It Matters: Life happens—babies are born, family members get sick. Paid leave means people don't have to choose between family and survival.

31. Police Accountability

- What It Is: Reforming policing practices and increasing transparency.

- Why It Matters: Trust in law enforcement is broken for many communities. Change ensures safety and fairness for everyone.

32. Reparations and Historical Justice

- What It Is: Acknowledging and addressing the wrongs of the past, like slavery and indigenous displacement.

- Why It Matters: Justice isn't just about the future—it's about healing the past. Reparations are a step toward righting historical wrongs.

33. Reproductive Health

- What It Is: Protecting access to contraception, abortion, and maternal care.

- Why It Matters: Reproductive rights are under attack. Defending them means empowering people to make choices about their own bodies.

34. Renewable Energy Transition

- What It Is: Shifting to clean energy sources like wind and solar.

- Why It Matters: Fossil fuels are destroying the planet. Renewable energy is the future, and your generation can lead the charge.

35. Racial and Social Justice

- What It Is: Confronting racism and creating a fair society for all.

- Why It Matters: Systemic inequality holds everyone back. Fighting for justice creates a world where everyone can thrive.

36. Refugee Rights

- What It Is: Protecting people forced to flee their homes due to war, persecution, or climate disasters.

- Why It Matters: Refugees are people with hopes and dreams, just like you. Welcoming them strengthens communities and reflects shared humanity.

37. Rural Development

- What It Is: Investing in small towns and rural communities.

- Why It Matters: Rural areas are often overlooked. Improving healthcare, internet, and education there builds a stronger nation for everyone.

38. Social Media Accountability

- What It Is: Regulating tech giants to combat misinformation and harmful content.

- Why It Matters: Social media shapes how we think and connect. Pushing for accountability ensures it's used responsibly.

39. Space Exploration and Regulation

- What It Is: Managing the rise of private space travel and the use of space resources.

- Why It Matters: Space is the new frontier, and how we manage it now will affect future generations. Your ideas could help guide how humanity explores responsibly.

40. Student Loan Debt

- What It Is: Reducing or canceling student loan debt and making education more affordable.

- Why It Matters: Student debt is crushing dreams. By tackling this issue, you're fighting for fair access to education and financial freedom.

41. Sustainable Fashion and Consumerism

- What It Is: Promoting ethical production practices and reducing waste in industries.

- Why It Matters: Fast fashion and overconsumption are harming the planet. Your choices can push brands toward sustainability.

42. Tax Reform

- What It Is: Fixing tax systems to ensure the wealthy pay their fair share.

- Why It Matters: When billionaires avoid taxes, the burden falls on you. Tax reform means funding education, health-care, and infrastructure fairly.

43. Technology in Education

- What It Is: Expanding access to digital tools for learning.

- Why It Matters: Not everyone has the technology they need to succeed. Bridging the gap ensures equal opportunity for all students.

44. Trade and Globalization

- What It Is: Ensuring global trade benefits workers, not just corporations.

- Why It Matters: Globalization shapes your job prospects and the cost of living. Smart policies create fairness in a connected world.

45. Universal Basic Income (UBI)

- What It Is: Guaranteeing a basic income for everyone to reduce poverty and insecurity.

- Why It Matters: UBI offers financial stability in a world of economic uncertainty. It's a radical idea whose time may have come.

46. Voting Rights and Electoral Reform

- What It Is: Protecting the right to vote and exploring new systems like ranked-choice voting.

- Why It Matters: Your vote is your power. Defending it ensures every voice is heard and elections are fair.

47. Water Rights and Access

- What It Is: Ensuring everyone has clean, safe water.

- Why It Matters: Water is life, but for many, it's not guaranteed. Protecting water access ensures a basic human right for all.

48. Women's Rights and Gender Equality

- What It Is: Fighting for equal pay, opportunities, and protections from violence.

- Why It Matters: Gender equality isn't just a women's issue—it's everyone's issue. Fairness benefits all of society.

49. Workers' Rights

- What It Is: Ensuring fair wages, safe workplaces, and the right to unionize.

- Why It Matters: Workers are the backbone of any economy. Fighting for their rights means a stronger, more just system.

50. Youth Empowerment and Civic Engagement

- What It Is: Encouraging young people to lead and participate in shaping the future.

- Why It Matters: You are the future. When young voices rise, innovation and progress follow.

Concluding Thoughts

Here's the thing: there's no one way to make a difference. You might love speaking up and leading rallies, or you might thrive quietly behind the scenes, researching and planning. Both roles—and everything in between—are essential.

So don't get stuck thinking, "I'm not the kind of person who can do this." You are or will be when you are ready. Whether you're a loudspeaker or a quiet powerhouse, there's a space for you to contribute authentically and meaningfully.

Change doesn't happen all at once. It happens when passionate people—like you—decide to take the first step. Find your spark. Follow it. The world needs what only you can bring.

How Change Begins

Change often begins in the wake of tragedy, when the pain of inaction becomes too much to bear. That's exactly what happened after the shooting at Marjory Stoneman Douglas High School in Parkland, Florida, on February 14, 2018. Seventeen lives were lost that day, and the survivors could have easily been overwhelmed by grief.

Instead, a group of students decided that enough was enough. Tired of seeing lawmakers offer thoughts and prayers without action, they channeled their heartbreak into purpose. In the days after the shooting, students like Emma González, David Hogg, and Cameron Kasky took to social media, called out politicians, and demanded gun reform. From their frustration and passion, the March For Our Lives movement was born.

What started as a small group of teens determined to be heard quickly grew into a nationwide movement. On March 24, 2018, just over a month after the shooting, they organized one of the largest youth-led protests in U.S. history. Over 800,000 people gathered in Washington, D.C., with hundreds of sister marches worldwide. These were teenagers—kids who had been sitting in classrooms just weeks before—leading a global outcry for stricter gun laws.

Their message, "Enough is enough," resonated with millions, sparking a wave of voter registrations, policy conversations, and activism that continues to this day. They didn't just call for change; they inspired it by showing what's possible when passion meets persistence.

The Parkland students' story is a powerful reminder that you don't need to have all the answers to start making a difference. It's proof that anyone, no matter their age or experience, can create change when they care deeply enough to act. Their courage, organization, and refusal to stay silent transformed their grief into a movement that gave hope to millions.

Whether you thrive in the spotlight or prefer supporting others behind the scenes, there's a role for everyone in creating a better world. Change doesn't come from waiting—it begins the moment you decide to take a stand.

13

Caring for Yourself While Caring for Democracy

E ngaging in democracy is an act of hope—a belief in the possibility of a better world. Yet, democracy can feel like a marathon with no finish line. The problems are vast, progress is often incremental, and the weight of the world can feel crushing. But here's a truth that's as old as humanity itself: you can't help the world if you neglect yourself.

In the Buddhist tradition, there's an analogy that speaks directly to this tension. Imagine a raging river, full of people struggling against the current. Your instinct is to leap in and save them, but if you do, you'll likely be swept away too. To make a difference, you must keep your feet firmly planted on the shore, grounded in strength and stability. Only then can you reach out and help pull others to safety.

This wisdom is not just about saving others—it's about ensuring that you don't lose yourself in the process. Democracy needs you—not burned out, not overwhelmed, but steady and resilient. The world needs the best version of you, even if that means doing less to care for your mind, body, and spirit.

The Emotional Toll of Engagement

Democracy isn't for the faint of heart. It's messy, slow, and often disheartening. You might spend weeks or months advocating for a cause only to see a vote fall short. The systems that perpetuate inequality can feel unyielding, and setbacks can make it tempting to give up.

These feelings are natural. They're a sign that you care deeply, and that's a beautiful thing. But caring deeply also means recognizing your limits. If you push yourself to exhaustion, you'll have nothing left to give—to democracy, your community, or yourself.

Grounding Yourself: Keeping Your Feet on Solid Ground

The Buddhist analogy reminds us that we must stay grounded to be effective. Here's how to plant your feet firmly on the shore:

1. Care for Your Body

Your physical health is the foundation of your strength. Without it, your energy wanes, and even the smallest tasks can feel insurmountable.

- **Move:** Exercise doesn't have to be intense. A walk in nature, a yoga session, or even dancing in your living room can help release tension.

- **Rest:** Democracy will still be there tomorrow. Allow yourself to take breaks, sleep well, and recover.

- **Nourish:** Eat in a way that supports your energy and well-being. Treat food as fuel for the work ahead.

2. Care for Your Mind

An overstimulated mind can spiral into overwhelm, especially in the age of 24/7 news and social media.

- **Limit Inputs:** Choose when and how you consume information. Turn off alerts, take breaks from social media, and prioritize reliable sources.

- **Practice Mindfulness:** Techniques like meditation, deep breathing, or simply sitting quietly can calm the chaos in your mind.

- **Celebrate Small Wins:** Don't wait for sweeping victories. A kind conversation, a single voter registered, or a local issue addressed are all steps forward.

3. Care for Your Spirit

Your spirit is the source of your hope, creativity, and resilience.

- **Connect:** Surround yourself with people who inspire and uplift you. Share your worries and victories with those who understand.

- **Reflect:** Keep a journal to process your thoughts and emotions. Writing can bring clarity and lighten the emotional load.

- **Engage in Joy:** Democracy is important, but so is laughter, art, and moments of unfiltered joy. These aren't distractions—they're fuel.

The Power of Doing Less

In a culture that celebrates doing more, it can feel counterintuitive to slow down. But sometimes, doing less allows you to do more in the long run. When you step back to care for yourself, you return stronger, clearer, and more effective.

Remember: the world doesn't need a burned-out version of you. It needs the version of you who can think creatively, lead with empathy, and persevere through challenges. If that means saying no to one more meeting, skipping a rally to rest, or taking a break from advocacy to recharge, you're not failing—you're preparing.

Reframing Success

Progress is slow, but every small action adds up. When you plant seeds, you might not see them bloom, but that doesn't mean they won't. Trust in the process, and remember that you're part of a larger ecosystem of people working toward change.

Questions to Reflect On:

- What small victories can I celebrate today?

- What brings me joy, and how can I prioritize it?

- What can I let go of to protect my energy?

Concluding Thoughts

Democracy thrives on collective action, but it also depends on the strength of the individuals who show up for it. The best way to help others is to keep yourself steady and strong. When you care for your mind, body, and spirit, you embody the kind of resilience democracy needs.

So take a breath. Step back when you need to. And remember, the world needs the best of you—even if that means less. Because when you show up steady, grounded, and whole, your impact becomes immeasurable.

How Change Begins

Eleanor Roosevelt stepped into the role of First Lady in 1933, at a time when the nation was buckling under the weight of the Great Depression. For many, the position was largely ceremonial—hosting dinners, attending events, and staying out of the political fray. But Eleanor had no intention of standing idly by. She saw her role as an opportunity to shape the country's direction and give voice to those who were often overlooked. The work, however, was unrelenting, and Eleanor quickly realized that to serve others, she had to first care for herself.

Her sanctuary was a modest cottage called Val-Kill, tucked away in Hyde Park, New York. It was here, far from the demands of Washington and the glare of public scrutiny, that Eleanor found her footing. Val-Kill wasn't luxurious; it wasn't grand. But it was hers—a space where she could think, recharge, and reconnect with her purpose. She would sit by the window, the soft rustle of leaves outside, and let her thoughts spill onto the pages of her journal. Writing gave her clarity. It was a private dialogue, a way to make sense of the noise around her and the quiet voice within.

When the weight of her responsibilities became overwhelming, Eleanor would take long walks through the woods surrounding her cottage. The crunch of leaves underfoot, the cool air against her skin—these simple, grounding moments reminded her of the beauty and resilience of the natural world. They were a balm for her spirit, a quiet reminder that even amidst turmoil, there was still harmony to be found.

Eleanor didn't retreat into solitude entirely, though. She understood the importance of connection, of drawing strength from those who shared her vision. At Val-Kill, she often hosted intimate gatherings with close friends and advisors. They would sit around the table, sharing simple meals and deep conversations. These weren't grand political strategizing sessions; they were moments of mutual support and inspiration. Eleanor valued the laughter, the encouragement, and the perspective these friends brought into her life. They reminded her that she wasn't alone in her efforts.

Even as she recharged in these quiet ways, Eleanor kept her connection to the public alive through her daily newspaper column, My Day. Writing wasn't just a way to process her own thoughts; it was a way to reach others, to share her hopes, her frustrations, and her belief in the power of small actions. Through her words, she inspired millions, but the act of writing also sustained her, giving her a sense of purpose even when progress seemed slow.

As the years went on, the demands of her position only grew. World War II brought new challenges, new sorrows, and an even greater need for her advocacy. Yet, through it all, Eleanor held onto her practices of self-care. They were what allowed her to remain a steady, reliable force in the face of chaos. She didn't see these moments of rest as indulgences; she saw them as necessities.

Eleanor often said that the future belongs to those who believe in the beauty of their dreams. What she didn't always say was that dreams require stamina, and stamina requires care. Her quiet time at Val-Kill, her walks, her writing, her connections with friends—all of these were acts of self-preservation that allowed her to carry the immense weight of her work.

Eleanor's story is a reminder that to make a lasting impact, you must first sustain yourself. You can't pour from an empty cup, and you can't pull others from the river if you're swept away yourself. When the world feels overwhelming and the work seems endless, think of Eleanor in her small cottage, taking the time to care for her mind, body, and spirit. It wasn't just how she survived—it was how she thrived. And because she thrived, so did the causes she championed, leaving a legacy of strength and compassion that continues to inspire.

Eleanor Roosevelt's unwavering commitment to self-care was not just a personal necessity—it became a model of sustainability for leaders and advocates everywhere. By balancing her tireless public service with moments of reflection, connection, and rejuvenation, she demonstrated that enduring change requires enduring strength.

Her ability to step back, ground herself, and tend to her own well-being allowed her to return to her work with clarity and resilience, inspiring countless others to follow suit. From activists like Marian Wright Edelman to modern leaders like Michelle Obama, Eleanor's example serves as a reminder that caring for oneself is not a retreat from responsibility but a vital act of empowerment. Through her life, she showed that the best way to serve others is to first ensure you remain steady, strong, and ready to act—a lesson that continues to resonate across generations.

14

Bringing It All Together—How Democracy Thrives

D emocracy isn't just a system of government—it's a living, breathing thing. It grows, adapts, and thrives with care. Like a vibrant garden, democracy needs attention and nurturing. It relies on planting seeds of hope, watering them with collective action, and weeding out misinformation, apathy, and division. But here's the truth: democracy doesn't just survive on its own. It thrives because of us—because of you.

Think about this journey we've taken together. Along the way, we've uncovered the transformative power of showing up, the joy of discovering your passion, and the strength that comes from standing together. Democracy reflects the care it receives, and every action you take strengthens its roots, helping it grow stronger and more resilient.

In moments of uncertainty, it's easy to feel small, to wonder if your contributions matter. But history tells a different story. Time and again, we've seen how ordinary people stepping into their extraordinary power have transformed the world. The civil rights movement didn't happen because a single person made it so—it happened because countless individuals refused to give up on the promise of equality. Women's suffrage wasn't handed to us; it was fought for by people who believed that their voices deserved to be heard. Marriage equality didn't come about overnight—it was built through stories, persistence, and a belief in love's transformative power.

Our democracy today faces challenges, just as it always has. Misinformation clouds the truth. Division threatens to pull us apart. Apathy whispers, Does it even matter? But we know better. We know that democracy's greatest strength is its people—people who show up, speak out, and refuse to let cynicism take root.

Imagine democracy as a garden again. Every action you take is a seed. Maybe it's a small one—like a conversation with a neighbor, a single vote, or an email to a representative. Or maybe it's something bigger—organizing a community effort, joining a movement, or leading change in your own unique way. Each seed matters because together, they grow into something far greater than the sum of their parts. And when that garden blooms, it's not just beautiful—it's powerful.

Tending to democracy isn't all hard work. There's joy in it, too. The pride you feel when you see progress. The connection you find with others who share your vision. The sense of purpose that grows as you align your actions with your values. These moments remind us why democracy is worth every ounce of effort. Caring for it doesn't just strengthen the system—it strengthens us. It connects us to each other, builds our communities, and gives us a reason to hope.

Here's where it all comes together: this is your moment. Not the end of the journey, but the beginning. The story of democracy isn't written by someone else—it's written by us. Your voice matters. Your actions matter. Every time you show up, you're shaping a future that reflects the best of who we are and what we can be.

Don't wait for someone else to fix it. Don't sit on the sidelines hoping for the perfect leader or the ideal moment. The moment is now, and the leader we've been waiting for? It's all of us.

So step forward—not perfectly, not all at once, but consistently. Start small if you need to. Start big if you're ready. Just start. Plant your seeds, water them with care, and trust that they'll grow. Together, we can create a thriving democracy that reflects our highest hopes and deepest values. Together, we can build a world that's fairer, kinder, and full of possibility.

This is our moment to embrace the living spirit of democracy, to nurture it, and to help it flourish. The future isn't something we wait for—it's something we shape with every choice we make, every action we take, every seed we plant.

You've got what it takes. The world we want tomorrow depends on what we do today. So go ahead, take that first step, and keep going.

The garden is waiting for us to tend it. The future is waiting for us to build it. Let's get to work. Together.

How Change is Beginning

The story of the Equal Rights Amendment (ERA) is another testament to democracy's potential—and its challenges. It's a story of progress, setbacks, and the enduring belief that equality under the law should be guaranteed for all. While the ERA remains unfinished, its journey offers valuable lessons about persistence, collective action, and the ongoing work of democracy.

The ERA was first introduced to Congress in 1923 by suffragist Alice Paul, just three years after the 19th Amendment granted women the right to vote. Paul envisioned the ERA as the next step in securing equality, a constitutional guarantee that rights would not be denied or abridged on account of sex. Her vision was clear, but the road ahead was anything but.

For decades, the ERA languished in Congress, with opponents arguing that it was unnecessary or even dangerous. Women's rights advocates, however, continued to push forward. The women's liberation movement of the 1960s and 1970s reignited the fight, bringing the ERA back into the national spotlight. In 1972, nearly 50 years after it was first introduced, Congress finally passed the ERA, sending it to the states for ratification.

The amendment needed the approval of 38 states to become part of the Constitution. At first, momentum was strong—22 states ratified it within the first year. But opposition mounted, led by figures like Phyllis Schlafly, who argued that the ERA would dismantle traditional gender roles and harm families. Misconceptions and fear campaigns slowed the amendment's progress, and by the 1982 deadline, it had been ratified by only 35 states, three short of the required number.

The fight for the ERA could have ended there. But democracy, like its advocates, is resilient. In recent years, the movement has gained new energy. Nevada ratified the ERA in 2017, Illinois followed in 2018, and Virginia became the 38th state to ratify it in 2020. These victories have reignited hope and raised questions about whether the deadline for ratification should be extended or removed altogether.

The unfinished story of the ERA reminds us that democracy is not a straight line. Progress often comes in fits and starts, with victories and setbacks along the way. But it also shows us the power of persistence. For nearly a century, advocates have kept the fight alive, planting seeds of equality in every generation. Each step—every speech, march, and legislative push—has brought the nation closer to fulfilling the promise of equal rights for all.

It also highlights the importance of collective action. The ERA has been championed by people from all walks of life—women and men, young and old, from every corner of the country. Their efforts underscore a fundamental truth about democracy: it thrives when we show up, together, to demand a better future.

The ERA's story is still being written. It asks us to consider what kind of nation we want to be. Do we want a Constitution that states women have all rights afforded to men in our country, or one that leaves those principles open to interpretation? Do we want to continue the work of those who fought before us, or let their efforts fade into history?

This unfinished chapter is a call to action. It's a reminder that democracy requires care, persistence, and courage. The fight for the ERA may not be over, but its legacy is already clear: every step forward, no matter how small, brings us closer to a nation where equality is not just an ideal but a reality.

The Equal Rights Amendment reminds us that democracy isn't static—it's a living thing, shaped by the people who nurture it. And while the ERA's journey remains incomplete, it stands as proof that the work of democracy is never finished—but always worth pursuing.

Share Your Thoughts

I magine this book, sitting out there in the world, ready to inspire and spark action. But without reviews, it's like a musician playing to an empty room or a chef creating a masterpiece that no one tastes. A book without reviews doesn't get the chance to connect with others—it just sits there, quietly waiting.

That's where you come in. Reviews don't just tell people about the book; they start conversations, open doors, and let others know what to expect. Whether it's a quick note about what you loved or a few lines about how it resonated with you, your words could help someone else decide to give it a read.

It's easy to do—just scan the QR code, and you'll be taken straight to where you can leave a review. Think of it as a small way to pay it forward for the next reader.

This book was written to make a difference, and your review can help it reach the people who need it most. Thanks for taking the time—and for making it all the way to the end!

1. Federal Election Commission, "Overview of Elections and Campaign Regulations," accessed https://www.fec.gov.
National Conference of State Legislatures, "Local Election Dynamics," accessed https://www.ncsl.org/research/elections-and-campaigns.aspx.

2. Brennan Center for Justice, "Elections and Voting Rights," accessed https://www.brennancenter.org.
FairVote, "The Role of the Popular Vote in State Elections," accessed https://www.fairvote.org.

3. Brookings Institution, "National Mandates and Policy Priorities," accessed https://www.brookings.edu.
Jeffrey Tulis, "The Mandate Game: How Popular Votes Shape Political Agendas," Brookings Institution.

4. National Archives and Records Administration, "Understanding the Electoral College," accessed https://www.archives.gov/electoral-college.
Pew Research Center, "Public Opinion on the Electoral College and Voting Trends," accessed https://www.pewresearch.org.

5. Harvard Kennedy School, "Redistricting, Voter Turnout, and Policy Impact," accessed https://www.hks.harvard.edu.

6. Deci, Edward L., and Ryan, Richard M. "Self-Determination Theory and the Facilitation of Intrinsic Motivation, Social Development, and Well-Being." *American Psychologist,* 55, no. 1 (2000): 68–78.

7. The Lancet, "Purpose in Life and Health Outcomes," accessed at The Lancet.

8. McGonigal, Kelly. *The Upside of Stress: Why Stress Is Good for You, and How to Get Good at It* (New York: Avery, 2015).

9. Deci, Edward L., and Ryan, Richard M. "Self-Determination Theory and the Facilitation of Intrinsic Motivation, Social Development, and Well-Being." *American Psychologist,* 55, no. 1 (2000): 68–78.

10. Angela Duckworth, *Grit: The Power of Passion and Perseverance* (New York: Scribner, 2016).

11. Malala Yousafzai, *I Am Malala: The Girl Who Stood Up for Education and Was Shot by the Taliban* (London: Weidenfeld & Nicolson, 2013).

About the Author

Bonnie A. Ross

Identity Coach | Energy Mentor | Author

Bonnie A. Ross is a renowned life coach, energy mentor, gifted poet, and the founder of Presently Me Coaching, with a prolific career spanning over three decades. Throughout her 35 years in the field, Bonnie has devoted herself to helping people navigate significant life transitions, assisting them in recognizing and embracing their evolving selves. Her approach uniquely combines energy work with personal growth, providing a refined journey for individuals at the threshold of new beginnings.

Bonnie's career began with her compassionate work as an energy practitioner, where she used touch therapy to offer comfort to AIDS patients. This early experience laid the foundation for her life-long commitment to energy healing. Over time, Bonnie expanded her expertise to include meditation for pain relief, advanced life coaching, and Reiki mastery, showcasing her exceptional skill in addressing the energy blockages that often arise from life's challenges.

Her extensive experience also extends into the corporate world, where she spent over 25 years, including 18 years as an executive at The Walt Disney Company. This background infuses her coaching with a distinctive blend of business acumen and spiritual insight, enhancing her ability to guide both personal and professional development. As a certified Senior HR professional and a small business entrepreneur, Bonnie possesses a comprehensive view of growth and success.

Bonnie is also a deeply insightful author whose works reflect her profound connection to nature. Her poetry and writings capture the intricate interrelations of nature, its continuous renewal, and its acceptance of change. This perspective offers her readers and clients a viewpoint that is both resilient and harmonious.

Living in the serene Blue Ridge Mountains of Buncombe County, North Carolina, with Edison, her rescue dog, Bonnie's life is a testament to her belief in the transformative power of nature's peace and beauty. Her existence amidst such tranquility fuels her work, serving as a constant reminder that life's fluctuations are ripe with opportunities for growth and self-exploration. Bonnie A. Ross is more than a coach, author, or poet; she is a guiding light for anyone searching for their place in the world.

Also by Bonnie A Ross

Showing Up For Democracy
Break Through Doubt, Leverage the Popular
Vote, and Shape Our Future

Poetry Inspired Journaling
Unlock Creative Flow, Emotional Release,
and Daily Inspiration with the Power of Verse

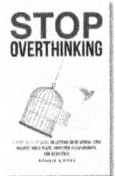

Stop Overthinking
A Step-by-Step Guide to Letting Go of Mental
Spin to Achieve Inner Peace, Improved
Relationships, and Resilience

Stop Overthinking for Leaders
A Leading-Edge Guide to Decisive
Leadership, Empowering Teams and Driving
Strategic Alignment

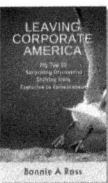

Leaving Corporate America
My Top 10 Surprising Discoveries Shifting from
Executive to Entrepreneur